I0583682

DISCARDED FROM
GARFIELD COUNTY
LIBRARIES

Garfield County Libraries
Rifle Branch Library
207 East Ave
Rifle, CO 81650
(970) 625-3471 • Fax (970) 625-3549
www.GCPLD.org

Stephenie Meyer

WHO
WROTE
THAT?

LOUISA MAY ALCOTT

JANE AUSTEN

AVI

L. FRANK BAUM

JUDY BLUME,
    SECOND EDITION

BETSY BYARS

MEG CABOT

BEVERLY CLEARY

ROBERT CORMIER

BRUCE COVILLE

ROALD DAHL

CHARLES DICKENS

ERNEST J. GAINES

THEODOR GEISEL

S.E. HINTON

WILL HOBBS

ANTHONY HOROWITZ

STEPHEN KING

MADELEINE L'ENGLE

GAIL CARSON LEVINE

C.S. LEWIS

LOIS LOWRY

ANN M. MARTIN

STEPHENIE MEYER

L.M. MONTGOMERY

PAT MORA

WALTER DEAN MYERS

ANDRE NORTON

SCOTT O'DELL

BARBARA PARK

KATHERINE PATERSON

GARY PAULSEN

RICHARD PECK

TAMORA PIERCE

DAVID "DAV" PILKEY

EDGAR ALLAN POE

BEATRIX POTTER

PHILIP PULLMAN

MYTHMAKER:
    THE STORY OF
    J.K. ROWLING,
    SECOND EDITION

MAURICE SENDAK

SHEL SILVERSTEIN

GARY SOTO

JERRY SPINELLI

R.L. STINE

EDWARD L.
    STRATEMEYER

E.B. WHITE

LAURA INGALLS
    WILDER

LAURENCE YEP

JANE YOLEN

Stephenie Meyer

Tracey Baptiste

Foreword by
Kyle Zimmer

CHELSEA HOUSE
PUBLISHERS
An imprint of Infobase Publishing

Stephenie Meyer

Copyright © 2010 by Infobase Publishing

All rights reserved. No part of this book may be reproduced or utilized in any form or by any means, electronic or mechanical, including photocopying, recording, or by any information storage or retrieval systems, without permission in writing from the publisher. For information, contact:

Chelsea House
An imprint of Infobase Publishing
132 West 31st Street
New York, NY 10001

Library of Congress Cataloging-in-Publication Data
Baptiste, Tracey.
Stephenie Meyer / Tracey Baptiste.
 p. cm. — (Who wrote that?)
Includes bibliographical references and index.
ISBN 978-1-60413-693-7
1. Meyer, Stephenie, 1973—Juvenile literature. 2. Authors, American—21st century—Biography—Juvenile literature. 3. Young adult fiction—Authorship—Juvenile literature. I. Baptiste, Tracey. II. Title.
 PS3613.E979Z59 2010
 813'.6—dc22
 [B]   2009022861

Chelsea House books are available at special discounts when purchased in bulk quantities for business, associations, institutions, or sales promotions. Please call our Special Sales Department in New York at (212) 967-8800 or (800) 322-8755.

You can find Chelsea House on the World Wide Web at http://www.chelseahouse.com

Text design by Keith Trego and Erika K. Arroyo
Cover design by Alicia Post
Composition by EJB Publishing Services
Cover printed by Bang Printing, Brainerd, MN
Book printed and bound by Bang Printing, Brainerd, MN
Date printed: April 2010
Printed in the United States of America

10 9 8 7 6 5 4 3 2 1

This book is printed on acid-free paper.

All links and Web addresses were checked and verified to be correct at the time of publication. Because of the dynamic nature of the Web, some addresses and links may have changed since publication and may no longer be valid.

Table of Contents

FOREWORD BY
KYLE ZIMMER
PRESIDENT, FIRST BOOK   6

1   RISE OF THE VAMPIRE AUTHOR   11

2   THE EARLY YEARS   21

3   DAWN OF THE WRITER   33

4   LURED BY TWILIGHT   43

5   OVER THE MOON   53

6   ECLIPSING RECORDS   61

7   BREAKING MOLDS   71

8   HER OWN BRAND OF VAMPIRE   83

9   BEYOND BOOKS   97

CHRONOLOGY   106
NOTES   107
WORKS BY STEPHENIE MEYER   114
POPULAR BOOKS   115
POPULAR CHARACTERS   116
MAJOR AWARDS   117
BIBLIOGRAPHY   118
FURTHER READING   123
INDEX   124

FOREWORD BY
KYLE ZIMMER
PRESIDENT, FIRST BOOK

HUMANITY IS POWERED by stories. From our earliest days as thinking beings, we employed every available tool to tell each other stories. We danced, drew pictures on the walls of our caves, spoke, and sang. All of this extraordinary effort was designed to entertain, recount the news of the day, explain natural occurrences—and then gradually to build religious and cultural traditions and establish the common bonds and continuity that eventually formed civilizations. Stories are the most powerful force in the universe; they are the primary element that has distinguished our evolutionary path.

Our love of the story has not diminished with time. Enormous segments of societies are devoted to the art of storytelling. Book sales in the United States alone topped $24 billion in 2006; movie studios spend fortunes to create and promote stories; and the news industry is more pervasive in its presence than ever before.

There is no mystery to our fascination. Great stories are magic. They can introduce us to new cultures, or remind us of the nobility and failures of our own, inspire us to greatness or scare us to death; but above all, stories provide human insight on a level that is unavailable through any other source. In fact, stories connect each of us to the rest of humanity not just in our own time, but also throughout history.

This special magic of books is the greatest treasure that we can hand down from generation to generation. In fact, that spark in a child that comes from books became the motivation for the creation of my organization, First Book, a national literacy program with a simple mission: to provide new books to the most disadvantaged children. At present, First Book has been at work in hundreds of communities for over a decade. Every year children in need receive millions of books through our organization and millions more are provided through dedicated literacy institutions across the United States and around the world. In addition, groups of people dedicate themselves tirelessly to working with children to share reading and stories in every imaginable setting from schools to the streets. Of course, this Herculean effort serves many important goals. Literacy translates to productivity and employability in life and many other valid and even essential elements. But at the heart of this movement are people who love stories, love to read, and want desperately to ensure that no one misses the wonderful possibilities that reading provides.

When thinking about the importance of books, there is an overwhelming urge to cite the literary devotion of great minds. Some have written of the magnitude of the importance of literature. Amy Lowell, an American poet, captured the concept when she said, "Books are more than books. They are the life, the very heart and core of ages past, the reason why men lived and worked and died, the essence and quintessence of their lives." Others have spoken of their personal obsession with books, as in Thomas Jefferson's simple statement: "I live for books." But more compelling, perhaps, is the almost instinctive excitement in children for books and stories.

Throughout my years at First Book, I have heard truly extraordinary stories about the power of books in the lives of children. In one case, a homeless child, who had been bounced from one location to another, later resurfaced— and the only possession that he had fought to keep was the book he was given as part of a First Book distribution months earlier. More recently, I met a child who, upon receiving the book he wanted, flashed a big smile and said, "This is my big chance!" These snapshots reveal the true power of books and stories to give hope and change lives.

As these children grow up and continue to develop their love of reading, they will owe a profound debt to those volunteers who reached out to them—a debt that they may repay by reaching out to spark the next generation of readers. But there is a greater debt owed by all of us—a debt to the storytellers, the authors, who have bound us together, inspired our leaders, fueled our civilizations, and helped us put our children to sleep with their heads full of images and ideas.

WHO WROTE THAT? is a series of books dedicated to introducing us to a few of these incredible individuals. While we have almost always honored stories, we have not uniformly honored storytellers. In fact, some of the most important authors have toiled in complete obscurity throughout their lives or have been openly persecuted for the uncomfortable truths that they have laid before us. When confronted with the magnitude of their written work or perhaps the daily grind of our own, we can forget that writers are people. They struggle through the same daily indignities and dental appointments, and they experience the intense joy and bottomless despair that many of us do. Yet somehow they rise above it all to deliver a powerful thread that connects us all. It is a rare honor to have the opportunity that these books provide to share the lives of these extraordinary people. Enjoy.

The best-selling author Stephenie Meyer poses for a portrait in Beverly Hills, California, on November 8, 2008. Just a few years earlier, Meyer had been a stay-at-home mom with almost no writing experience.

1

Rise of the Vampire Author

THE UNSUSPECTING AUTHOR

"It wasn't a great time in my life. I'd put on so much weight with the two babies. My 30th birthday was coming up and I was so not ready to face being 30. I didn't feel I had much going for me. I had my kids, but there wasn't much I was doing,"[1] Stephenie Meyer recalled as she described the beginning of the summer of 2003. The previous year had also been hard on the family. She had broken her arm from a fall when she was pregnant with her youngest son, Eli. Five weeks after her fall, her husband was diagnosed with Crohn's disease, a chronic inflammation of the digestive tract. But all of this had occurred before she suddenly became a coveted author.

Meyer's luck turned one night when she was visited by a vampire. And as is custom in all vampire lore, by morning she was completely changed. Of course Meyer did not encounter an actual vampire. "I don't believe that vampires are real,"[2] Meyer is quick to point out. The vampire who came to her that night was in a dream that Meyer described as "an exceptional, one-of-a-kind, kind of dream."[3] The night before her sons were to have their first swimming lesson of the summer, she dreamed about a young vampire who loved a human girl and who worried about the fact that he was intoxicated by the smell of her blood and might not be able to resist biting her. Over that summer, she wrote a 130,000-word novel based on the two characters in that dream, and by the end of the year—breakneck speed in the publishing industry—Meyer had secured an agent and a whopping $750,000 three-book deal with a major publishing company, Little, Brown.

The first book, *Twilight*, was published in October 2005. Immediately, Meyer did all she could to promote the book. Little, Brown sent advanced readers' copies (ARC) of *Twilight* to booksellers; one of them made its way into the hands of Faith Hochhalter at Changing Hands Bookstore in Tempe, Arizona. Hochhalter said, "When I first got the ARC of *Twilight*, it was the first time since buying at Changing Hands that I read an ARC that I knew was going to be a huge hit." The next day, Hochhalter contacted Little, Brown to order more copies of the book. Then she gave her advance copy to other staff members at the bookstore and put Meyer on a panel to discuss young adult fiction at Changing Hands. "The first time that I met her, I have never been more nervous to meet an author in my whole life," Hochhalter said. "I was all shaking and nervous, and I had butterflies in my stomach. I loved the book so much, and I was so excited about selling this book."[4]

Meyer and Hochhalter became fast friends. Meyer would often go to the bookstore, which was not far from her own Arizona home, to sign copies of the book and meet Hochhalter for lunch. Because of Hochhalter's enthusiasm, Meyer's first signing at Changing Hands attracted about 80 people. That is an unusually large number for a first-time author. And from there, Hochhalter's enthusiastic word-of-mouth continued to spread.

THE VAMPIRE GOES VIRAL

Once the book was ready to be published, Little, Brown set up a Web site for *Twilight*. It was dark, in keeping with the book's theme. Meyer, however, was not happy with the site and decided to put up one of her own. She enlisted her younger brother Seth to be the Webmaster. The

Did you know...

According to a 2004 survey, only 14 percent of writers make enough money from their writing to cover their entire annual income. In the same survey, 54 percent of writers said they made nothing at all from their writing projects that year. The remaining writers supplemented whatever little writing money they earned with income from other jobs.

more sunny-looking site, available at http://www.stephenie meyer.com, is more than just about *Twilight*. There are two biography pages, a brief "official" one and a much longer "unofficial" one that tells about Meyer's life growing up in a large family. Meyer originally had her personal e-mail on the site so that fans could connect with her directly, but as her fame grew, she decided to take it down.

Little, Brown promoted the books vigorously in what some have called bold marketing moves. In addition to the Web site, they set up interviews with influential bloggers, issued press releases, and sent the books to major reviewers. In addition, Meyer went beyond the standard marketing on her own. "Stephenie was somebody who was early to use a new medium and to use it effectively," Tim O'Reilly, a technology expert, told the *Los Angeles Times*. "An authentic connection really matters."[5] Meyer found people online who were connecting with her books and characters and just started chatting with them. "In being so approachable and responsive, she unwittingly cemented her fledgling fan base, revealing herself as affable and human, surprised to have fans and genuinely delighted by their interest,"[6] reported Susan Carpenter. And in so doing, Meyer established herself, according to one reporter, as a "pop-culture sensation"[7] in the publishing industry at a time when many books were not selling well.

On her Web site, Meyer made not just herself, but also her family accessible, further making fans feel like part of her own clan. There were pictures of her sons on Halloween, dressed as a Power Ranger, Napoleon Dynamite, and Captain Hook. She included pictures of herself growing up in Arizona with her siblings. She also went beyond her own Web site, finding others where people had gathered online to discuss her books. Within a month of the book's release, fan sites began to appear. Brittany Gardener began a MySpace group in December 2006 after reading *Twilight* in one night. Meyer had, according to Heather Green, "never heard of MySpace, but once she discovered Gardener's group, she signed up. She started dropping in, answering fans' questions."[8] Some asked what kind of pet her main character Bella Swan might have and if it would be hard for her vampire boyfriend Edward Cullen to come around if she did. Another asked Meyer if she knew the percentage of vampires living in America.

Meyer found other fans who not only enjoyed her work, but had been inspired by it. Stay-at-home mother Lori Joffs began writing a version of *Twilight* from Edward's perspective and posted four chapters of her book on the Web site FanFiction.net. Meyer read the chapters and left Joffs a review saying, "I'm having a great time reading your version of things."[9] A thrilled Joffs then e-mailed Meyer, and the two struck up a fast friendship. Joffs wanted to delve into the meaning of words in the book, and so the number-one *Twilight* fan site was born, Twilight Lexicon. According to *BusinessWeek*, it draws about 30,000 daily visitors. Twilight Lexicon is so devoted to Meyer that the site's administrator will not comment on anything that is not pre-approved by Meyer or her publisher. (For example, the author's request for an interview for this biography garnered the following reply from an administrator: "Best wishes on your project, but we have a long standing policy of only commenting on official books put out by Stephenie's publisher, Little, Brown."[10])

Meyer also reached out to her fans outside of the virtual world. At a book signing, college student Kady Weatherford suggested that Meyer throw a prom. Meyer then formed a prom committee. She worked with Changing Hands Bookstore, Arizona State University's English department, and people she had connected with from all over the country to organize the event. Little, Brown had her announce the prom date just before the release of the second book in the series, *New Moon*. Tickets were just eight dollars, and they were gone in minutes. So Meyer added a second prom on the same day. Within hours, it also sold out. On May 5, 2007, 500 guests showed up for the party in prom dresses, and some with fake casts on their legs, channeling their inner, accident-prone Bella.

"In order to encourage people to come all fancy without worrying about being overdressed, I promised that my dress would out-formal every other dress in attendance,"[11] she wrote on her Web site. But Meyer found it very difficult to find an appropriate dress. Then, just a day before leaving the country for some author-related events, she found a red satin wedding gown in the window of a couture bridal shop. She bought it immediately and had 8 feet (2.4 meters) of train taken off and asked that a jacket be made with the extra fabric.

After the Eclipse Prom and the release of *Eclipse* in 2007, Meyer took her personal e-mail address off her Web site. She kept in touch through some exchanges on fan sites but was no longer directly accessible. In December 2007, she visited the fan site TwilightMOMS and expressed relief to find she was not the only mom "in love with fictional underage vampires and werewolves."[12] But Meyer continued to pull back her connection with fans. In July 2008, she asked that her top fan sites close discussions three weeks before *Breaking Dawn*, the final book in the

Twilight series, was released. She did not want fans discussing details from advanced copies before everyone had gotten a chance to read the books. Although she had found a home among her Internet fans, she was also burned when an unauthorized poster revealed a manuscript she was working on. Most of her fans understood Meyer's need to quell the overwhelming number of messages she received. Michelle Viera, another fan who started chatting via email with Meyer after the first book was published, told *BusinessWeek*, "She was open for fans to talk to. Now it's impossible. She's hugely busy."[13]

VAMPIRES ARE GOOD FOR THE ECONOMY

The vampire dynasty Meyer created has been good financially for both herself and Little, Brown (as well as its parent company, Hachette Book Group), but it has also helped a lot of other people. Many other merchandisers have decided to ride the wave of Meyer's success and cater to the vampire fans who love the books. Online T-shirt stores like Squidoo and Café Press started offering *Twilight* gear as soon as the series became popular in 2006. There is even *Twilight*-themed jewelry sold by online stores like Twilight Style. Twilight Style checked in at number 43 on the top *Twilight* fan sites, but they were not the only ones making glittery gear. Stiff competition allowed Meyer's fans to shop for bargains.

Despite wanting to show their love for the series, many fans found some items out of reach or were looking to be more frugal about their purchases. Many of Meyer's fans are turning to traditional discount retailers like WalMart for their *Twilight* gear, and chain retailers are happy to oblige. "By creating specially-dedicated *Twilight* stores, both in their brick-and-mortar locations and on their website, WalMart is creating a unique home for this beloved franchise's passionate fan base,"[14] said Steve Nickerson, president of Summit Home Entertainment, distributor of the *Twilight* movie.

Meyer's imaginary world has also created a host of spin-off books. Some have been written specifically about Meyer (including this one), while others have been written about her series, such as Lois Gresh's *The Twilight Companion: The Unauthorized Guide to the Series*. There has even been one by the director of the *Twilight* movie, Catherine Hardwicke, *Twilight*: *Director's Notebook*. Outside of the *Twilight* universe, publishers have sought to cash in on the popular vampire theme. "We've almost hit maximum for vampire books—I think there were about 27 in a one-year period,"[15] said a buyer at Bookazine, a wholesale buyer specializing in children's books. But Meyer stands firmly at the head of the pack. In fact, Meyer's popularity and economic influence is so tremendous that Little, Brown promoted

Did you know...

The publisher John Wiley & Sons, well known for their academic publications, has published two *Twilight*-themed test preparation books: *Defining Twilight: Vocabulary Workbook for Unlocking the SAT, ACT, GED, and SSAT* and *Defining New Moon: Vocabulary Workbook for Unlocking the SAT, ACT, GED, and SSAT*. Both were released in 2009.

editor Elizabeth Eulberg to serve as director of global publicity just for Stephenie Meyer!

Stephenie Meyer, a onetime stay-at-home mom, now leads a global market worth millions.

A circa 1840 portrait of the English novelist Charlotte Brontë (1816–1855), author of Jane Eyre *and sister to fellow writers Anne and Emily Brontë. Stephenie Meyer counts Charlotte Brontë among her favorite authors.*

2

The Early Years

FROM CONNECTICUT TO ARIZONA

The second of the six children (three girls followed by three boys), Stephenie Meyer was born Stephenie Morgan in Hartford, Connecticut, to Stephen and Candy Morgan, on December 24, 1973. Being born on Christmas Eve, Meyer admits, "has always given me a bad attitude toward birthdays in general."[1] In addition to the six kids and two adults in the house, the Morgans had a dog named Eagle. "I think that coming from such a large family has given me a lot of insight into different personality types—my siblings sometimes crop up as characters in my stories."[2] She thanks them on her Web site for allowing her to use their names and hopes that they are not disappointed with how their namesakes turned out.

The unusual spelling of Meyer's first name was her father's idea. "Stephen (+ ie = me)"[3] she writes on her Web site. Though her name was often misspelled before she became famous, she now finds the unusual spelling useful when she wants to Google herself.

Stephen and Candy Morgan, originally from the western United States, did not stay on the East Coast for long. Before Stephenie turned four, they moved to Phoenix, Arizona, where her father worked as the chief financial officer of a contracting firm. Although Meyer sunburns easily, she preferred the sunnier climate in Phoenix and now claims that she gets cold from any temperature below 75 degrees Fahrenheit (24 degrees Celsius).

HOME OF THE FIREBIRD

As a child, Meyer was an avid reader. "I read the fattest books I could get my hands on,"[4] she told Jaimee Rose in a 2007 interview for the *Arizona Republic*. Meyer's passion for the written word would aid her tremendously when she attended the prestigious Chaparral High School in Scottsdale. Chaparral, home of the Firebird, the school mascot, has a rigorous academic program with an extensive honors program. On her Web site, Meyer jokes that the football team "was renowned statewide—for their GPA."[5] The school regularly lands on *U.S. News & World Report*'s list of the best high schools in the country. Meyer was awarded a National Merit Scholarship while at Chaparral, which allowed her to pay for college.

But the school was not all academics, as Meyer reveals in her "unofficial" online biography. She remembers that some of the kids were wealthy and privileged. It was not unusual to see expensive cars, like Porsches, in the student parking lot or to find some girls return from summer vacation with new noses. Meyer, however, was not among this group. She has kept her original nose and did not own a car until she was in her twenties.

LITERARY LOVES

Meyer chose Brigham Young University (BYU) for her undergraduate degree. The college, owned by the Church of Jesus Christ of Latter-day Saints, is the largest religious university in the United States. Latter-day Saints members are also called Mormons. Because Meyer hailed from a Mormon family, BYU was an easy choice. When Meyer says that "on the list of the biggest party schools in the country, BYU consistently and proudly finishes dead last,"[6] she is not kidding. The college has a strict honor code and a conservative dress code that requires men to be clean shaven and women to be modestly attired.

Meyer majored in English at BYU but says she "concentrated on literature rather than creative writing, mostly because I didn't consider reading books as work (as long as I was going to be doing something anyway, I might as well get course credit for it, right?)."[7] "I don't know if I ever considered anything else. That's what I love. I love reading, and this was a major I could read in," she said. "I figured I'd go on and go to law school, but I wasn't super-concerned with supporting myself because I wasn't thinking beyond being a student."[8]

Meyer had many literary influences, but some of her favorite authors include fellow Mormon Orson Scott Card, who, like Meyer, has managed to reconcile being a popular author with his faith. She also cites classic literary influences such as William Shakespeare, Jane Austen, Louisa May Alcott, and Charlotte Brontë. The romantic ideas found in Meyer's own series reflect some of the themes found in the works of these authors.

FAMILY LIFE

In 1994, during the summer break before her senior year, Meyer met Christiaan "Pancho" Meyer. Although they were familiar with each other, they had never really spoken. Christiaan had just returned from a mission in Chile, where he worked to convert people to the Mormon faith. Although the two had attended the same Mormon church

Did you know...

Meyer grew up loving children's writers such as L.M. Montgomery, who wrote *Anne of Green Gables*, and Eva Ibbotson, author of *Journey to the River Sea* and *The Secret of Platform 13*. Among her more contemporary influences are Douglas Adams, best known for *The Hitchhiker's Guide to the Galaxy*, and Janet Evanovich, author of the *New York Times* best-selling Stephanie Plum series. It was through Evanovich's Web site that Meyer found her agency, Writers House.

since they were children, Stephenie does not recall them speaking even one word to each other until many years later. She says, "It's funny, because in 20 years of knowing each other, we never had a conversation. But we got along so well."[9] (The two had actually only known each other for 16 years. Meyer was 19 when they officially met.) Soon, the couple began to date.

"On our second official date was when he proposed," she says. "He proposed a lot. Over 40 times. He would propose every night and I would tell him 'no' every night. It was kind of our end-of-date thing. Mormons get married a lot faster. The no-sex thing does speed up relationships."[10] About nine months after their first real conversation, they were married.

Meyer then returned to BYU to finish her degree. After graduating in 1995 with a B.A. in literature, she moved with her new husband to Glendale, Arizona. She took a job as a receptionist, but it was not to last. Two years later, in 1997, they welcomed their first son, Gabe. Meyer quit her job to become a stay-at-home mother. Two more sons followed: Seth, born in 2000, and Eli in 2002. From then on, Meyer was occupied with being a mom, scrapbooking, making Halloween costumes, and the obligations of her church, which included three hours of services on Sunday, plus teaching a class for the 14- to 18-year-old children in her area. "It's not a church that's low on time commitments,"[11] she says.

THE CHURCH THAT SMITH BUILT

Meyer's faith has always been a big part of her life. "I am . . . a member of the Church of Latter-day Saints," Meyer writes on her Web site. "And that has a huge influence on

A significant religious and political figure of the 1830s and 1840s, Joseph Smith Jr. (1805–1844) was the founder of the Latter-day Saint movement, also known as Mormonism, the religion to which Stephenie Meyer belongs.

who I am and my perspective on the world, and therefore what I write."[12]

The Church of Latter-day Saints is a uniquely American religion that began in upstate New York. Unlike many religions that have very ancient origins, Mormonism is a modern religion that started about 200 years ago. In 1820, its founder, Joseph Smith Jr., was a 14-year-old boy living in Palmyra, New York, when he said he received a vision of Jesus and God together. Smith later wrote that while he had been praying for guidance about which church he should join, flesh-and-blood reincarnations of God and Jesus came to him and told him that no modern church followed the right path and that Smith would have to return to old church teachings if he wanted to follow the right path. He later indicated that an angel named Moroni directed him in finding gold plates that were buried on a hill near his home. Smith translated the text on the plates. His translation was published as the Book of Mormon on April 6, 1830. It was the beginning of a new religion.

MORMONISM IN *TWILIGHT*

"Her works should not be judged by her religious affiliation," said Don Evans, a spokesman for the Mormon Church in Phoenix, Arizona. "She could be Catholic, or Baptist, or atheist. It shouldn't matter."[13] But Meyer's religious affiliation does get a lot of airtime, and mostly from those of her own faith. "I get more of, 'What's a Mormon girl doing writing about vampires?' from the Mormon community than I do the outside."[14] Meyer admits that as she wrote, she was very concerned about what her friends at church would think of her books.

Fellow Mormon author Orson Scott Card offered Meyer some advice. He told her that it was impossible to please everyone. Some may say that her stories cross the line and that she cannot be a good Mormon and write certain things, while others will say that religion should not control the story. While the Mormon Church took no official position on the novels, Deseret Books, a Mormon-owned bookstore in Utah, took the Twilight series off the shelves in April 2009. The books would be available only through special order. The spokesperson for the store said it was standard procedure when a book was met with mixed reviews.

Religion and literature continued to clash as one woman reviewed *Twilight* and analyzed how it tied in to the Book of Mormon. Meyer said the reviewer was wrong on every point. It is undeniable, however, that her religion has influenced her writing. In the book *Mormon America*, the authors Richard and Joan Ostling describe a church that "stands uncompromisingly for chastity and moral responsibility."[15] Bella and Edward's romance has been described as "chaste" in many reviews. And by refusing to drink human blood, it is clear that Edward and the rest of the Cullen family were written with a moral core. "I never write messages,"[16] Meyer told *Time* in 2008, yet a few may have seeped in.

In *Twilight*, Edward discusses the origin of life:

Well, where did you come from? Evolution? Creation? Couldn't we have evolved in the same way as other species, predator and prey? Or, if you don't believe that all this world could have just happened on its own, which is hard for me to accept myself, is it so hard to believe that the same force that created the delicate angelfish with the shark, the baby seal and the killer whale, could create both our kinds together?[17]

While Edward's character does not admit that he believes in God, he does say that the concept of evolution is one that is hard for him to accept.

In *New Moon*, Carlisle, the paternal figure in the Cullen family, also says he believes in the existence of a higher power. "Never, in the nearly four hundred years now since I was born, have I ever seen anything to make me doubt whether God exists in some form or the other."[18] He goes on to say that he believes that there is hope for everyone—a basic truth in the Mormon faith. "I'm hoping that there is still a point to this life, even for us. It's a long shot, I'll admit. . . . By all accounts, we're damned regardless. But I hope, maybe foolishly, that we'll get some measure of credit for trying."[19]

In the third book, *Eclipse*, Bella finally comes up with a theory about why Edward refuses to attempt to have sex with her until after they are married. "You're trying to protect your virtue!"[20] Bella accuses Edward. He insists that it is not his virtue that he is trying to protect, but hers. His insistence on chastity is not about sex, but about her soul. He asks, "How many people in this room have a soul? A shot at heaven, or whatever there is after this life?" Though Bella firmly believes that Edward is not as damned as he believes, Edward concludes that "it might be too late for me."[21]

In *Breaking Dawn*, as Bella contemplates the end of her existence and that of the Cullens' as well, she thinks about whether any of them would experience an afterlife. "I wondered idly now and then if there would be anything for us on the other side. . . . I couldn't imagine it myself. On the other hand, I couldn't imagine Edward not existing somehow, somewhere."[22]

Even werewolf Jacob references the Bible during an argument with Bella. He reminds her of an Old Testament story in which two women come before King Solomon with a baby, asking the king to decide which one was the child's rightful mother. In the Twilight series, Bella is trapped between her love for Jacob and Edward and their love for her. Jacob felt that their opposing desires were pulling her apart. "I'm not going to cut you in half anymore, Bella,"[23] he said, referring to King Solomon's suggestion to cut the baby in half to end the argument between the women.

Despite these references to religion, Meyer insists there is only one deliberate injection of Mormon doctrine. Her favorite story from the Book of Mormon is about 2,000 stripling warriors from the Book of Alma. The parents of a small group of boys are under attack, but they have foresworn fighting because of their faith. Instead, the sons fight, and because the parents did not break their oath, the sons are spared from harm. In the series, Jacob and his wolf pack are the stripling warriors. Meyer explains: "In the history of the Book of Mormon, they would have been dark-skinned, the ancestors of the Native Americans who are here now. So for me, the Quileute are kind of these sons who have taken on the responsibility of taking care of their families."[24] Quileute is the tribe that Jacob belongs to in the books.

In the end, Meyer knows that her religion affects her writing. "When I'm writing the stories I'm just looking to have a good time. But I do think that because I'm a very religious person, it does tend to come out somewhat in the books, although always unconsciously."[25]

Two hikers explore the beautiful Hoh Rain Forest in the Olympic National Park in Washington State's westernmost region. In her dream, Stephenie Meyer pictured her two main characters meeting in such a forest.

3

Dawn of the Writer

DREAM OF A LIFETIME

June 2, 2003, should have been like any other day for Meyer. Her sons were going to have their first swimming lessons of the summer. She was supposed to start a new diet to lose the baby weight she had gained during her last pregnancy, but around four o'clock that morning, she woke up from a vivid dream.

"It was very clear. I was an observer. When I woke up, I sat there with my eyes closed, thinking about it. It was like reading a great book when you don't want to put it down; you want to know what happens next. So I just laid [sic] there, imagining."[1]

Unable to get the dream out of her mind, Meyer decided to write it down. Her first line became the opening line of Chapter 13 in *Twilight*. When the children woke up, she reluctantly took them to the pool. When they returned for lunch, she continued to write again. By the end of the day, she had 10 pages. And then she was not able to stop.

The dream that became the first chapter Meyer wrote centered on a woman and her lover talking in a dense green forest, and the man was beautiful and glittering. He was a vampire. Their conversation focused on the difficulties of a human-vampire relationship in which, as Meyer explains, "A) they were falling in love with each other while B) the vampire was particularly attracted to the scent of her blood, and was having a difficult time restraining himself from killing her immediately."[2]

WORKING OBSESSIVELY

"There was a lot of pleasure in that first writing experience. It felt like a dam bursting, there was so much that I couldn't get out, and then I could," Meyer says of the start of her writing life. After that, she spent hours every day at the computer writing the story of the lovers who had appeared in her dream. "It sounds so cheesy,"[3] Meyer says of the transition from dream to printed page. Because she had no idea who the people in her dream were, she called them "he" and "she." But when she had finished transcribing her dream, the characters just kept on talking. The dream had not ended.

"The greatest challenge was finding time away from my already full life. I became somewhat of a hermit that summer, neglecting friends, family, and my normal hobbies," Meyer says. But she wrote often, "scribbling on the corners of envelopes and napkins, anything I could get my hands on so I wouldn't forget."[4] While she was taking the boys to their swimming lessons, she would plot, and she would write as soon as she got back home to the computer and had a spare moment. She wrote mostly at night while the kids were asleep before finally dragging herself to bed, exhausted, only to find that the characters still had more to say. Eventually, Meyer started keeping a notebook next to her bed that she would write in at night when more of the story came. In the morning, she would try to decipher her midnight scratchings and transcribe them into the story.

Meyer says the way she worked was obsessive. As she wrote *Twilight*, she made no use of outline or a synopsis; she just let the story take over and wrote it as it came. She was also obsessive about keeping what she was doing from her family. Her husband started to ask what she was up to and why he could never use the computer. "I was really protective and shy about it because it's a vampire romance. It's still embarrassing to say those words," she says. "It's not like I was going to tell him that I was writing this story about vampires, because he was just going to be even more perturbed." The two got into little arguments, but Meyer says that was normal. "We argue all the time because that's our personalities," she says. "We didn't get in mean arguments, but I'm sure we argued over it because we argue about everything—we argue about milk."[5]

Eventually, her sister Emily Rasmussen managed to get the story out of her. She said it was strange that Meyer was not talking to her, so she called and asked what was going on. Meyer says she took a deep breath and blurted it out. She had never kept secrets from her sister before. "I was ashamed to tell her because it was a vampire story,"[6] Meyer says. But it turned out that her sister was a fan of *Buffy the*

Vampire Slayer, a television series that followed vampire slayer Buffy Summers on her quest to bring an end to the undead. Her sister wanted to see what she had written, and Meyer e-mailed a couple of chapters to her. Rasmussen loved every word. Soon, Meyer was sending her sister whatever she wrote. Rasmussen said that she called and begged her sister all the time for new pages.

As she wrote more of her vampire story, Meyer realized that her characters needed names. For the male vampire, she went back to her literary studies. She chose Edward, an homage to Charlotte Brontë's Mr. Rochester from *Jane Eyre* and Jane Austen's Mr. Ferrars from *Sense and Sensibility*. She wanted a name that had a romantic feel, but one that had fallen out of popularity in recent years. With the vampire named, she turned to naming the heroine. She felt very possessive of the character, almost as if she were her own child, so Meyer decided to give her the name that she had been saving for a daughter, if she had had one. That was how Isabella (Bella) Swan was finally born.

For her lush, green, waterlogged setting, Meyer turned to Google for research. She needed some place that was "ridiculously rainy,"[7] she says. Google led her to Washington State. Then she searched through the maps to find a small, out-of-the-way town that was surrounded by dense forest. She found Forks, Washington, and thought it was built especially for her story.

When she wrote the end of the story, she turned back to the beginning to describe how the lovers had gotten to the conversation that had come to Meyer in her dream, which was now the middle of her tale. The beginning of the story finally caught up to the middle in August, three months after she first dreamed up her characters and their romantic meeting in the forest. Her writing consumed her, but she was still a mom first. "I can't close doors and write. Even if the kids are asleep, I know that I could hear them if I needed. I feel better if I'm kind of in the center of things and I know what's going on."[8]

STAKING A CLAIM

Meyer still was unsure of what she had on her hands. At 500 manuscript pages, she realized that what she had written was long enough to be called a book. Her older sister was the only person who knew what she was up to, and she encouraged Meyer to find a publisher. But Meyer found the process difficult. "You don't wrap it up in brown paper like they do in the movies," she said. "It looked like you needed to get an agent, which was very intimidating."[9] Once she was let in on the secret, Meyer's sister Heidi directed her to best-selling author Janet Evanovich's Web site. There, Meyer found the literary agency Writers House. She decided to write 15 query letters, asking 10 agencies (including Writers House) and five publishers if they wanted to see her manuscript, which she titled *Forks*. And then she waited, but not for long.

Did you know...

Each of Meyer's books has an accompanying playlist that she posts on her Web site. This music inspired her writing and helps to bring about the right feel for each part of the book. Meyer feels that the music is very indicative of the plot of each book, so she does not release the playlist until the books are released, for fear the songs will create spoilers for her readers.

The British writer Mary Wollstonecraft Shelley (1797–1851) was the author of Frankenstein, *one of the most famous horror stories of all time. Like Stephenie Meyer, Shelley based her novel on a dream.*

An assistant named Genevieve at Writers House responded to her query letter and asked to see the first three chapters of *Forks*. Meyer was nervous about sending them to her, believing that the first three chapters were weak in comparison to the rest of the story, but Genevieve loved them. She wanted the full manuscript. It was the first time that publication seemed a reality to Meyer.

A month later, Meyer had an agent. Jodi Reamer responded after reading the manuscript and asked to take Meyer on as a client. The two immediately got to work. For two weeks, they worked on tweaking the manuscript before sending it out to publishers. First on the agenda was finding a new title. Meyer still liked *Forks*, but Reamer insisted on something more in-tune with the nature of the story. They finally settled on *Twilight*. Manuscripts were sent to about nine different publishing houses in the fall of 2003. By November, Meyer and Reamer had their first bite.

As Reamer began sending Meyer's manuscript to publishing houses, other literary agencies responded to Meyer's initial query. Some wanted to see more, some rejected the manuscript, and one even rejected it after reading just the first chapter. But there was one rejection in particular that

Did you know...

Meyer is not the first author who had a dream that turned into a successful book. Mary Shelley, the author of *Frankenstein*, said that she originally dreamed about Frankenstein and the monster he had pieced together. Shelley, then 18, and her soon-to-be husband, Percy Bysshe Shelley, were spending the summer at the home of the British poet Lord Byron. Due to inclement weather, the three stayed inside and read ghost stories. Then they wrote their own. Shelley intended *Frankenstein* to be a short story, but with Percy's encouragement, it became a novel. It was published the following year, on January 1, 1818.

incensed Meyer. "The meanest rejection I got came *after* Little, Brown had [bought the book], so it didn't bother me at all," she wrote on her Web site, although it clearly did. She went on to say, "I'll admit that I considered sending back a copy of that rejection stapled to the write-up my deal got in *Publishers Weekly*, but I took the higher road."[10]

How had Meyer gotten a book deal? Megan Tingley, the head of her own division of Little, Brown, got hold of the manuscript before heading out on a cross-country plane trip over Thanksgiving weekend. She read it on the plane and immediately saw that it had vast potential. Tingley admitted that she was not one to publish genre fiction, as Meyer's vampire romance was. In fact, Meyer had pitched the book as a vampire-horror-romance story, even though there was not much of a horror element. But Tingley felt that the characters had universal appeal. "It might sound trite, but I've been in this business for 20 years and it's rare when you read something and just know. . . . These books have every element of a totally satisfying blockbuster,"[11] Tingley remarked in an interview with *Publishers Weekly* in 2007. She said that she could not wait for the plane to land so she could sign the book. The following Monday when she returned to work after the holiday, Tingley contacted Reamer with a $350,000 offer. Reamer turned it down and asked for a million.

"I almost threw up,"[12] Meyer said, when she learned of Reamer's refusal.

But Meyer's agent was right. Her novel was soon the center of a bidding war between publishing houses. Eventually, Tingley convinced her bosses at Little, Brown to up the ante, offering $750,000 for three books. It was the largest amount they had ever offered a new writer. Reamer happily accepted. The day in December Reamer called Meyer to tell her of the sale felt surreal to Meyer. She said she tried to remain professional while she was on the phone with her agent, but she was unable to maintain the façade for long. Immediately afterward, she called her sister, and Meyer's youngest son followed her around with his play phone imitating her nervous laughter.

In seven months, Meyer had gone from a housewife with a dream to the Cinderella of the publishing industry. "My life twisted around into 'I have an agent,' 'I have a book deal,' 'I have a career' and 'Wow, I'm going to be a writer, how odd is that?'"[13] Meyer said. Early on, Meyer recognized her unlikely luck and how others might react to it. In an interview for the *Seattle Post-Intelligencer* in 2005, she admitted, "Other writers are going to hate me."[14]

In the 2008 film adaptation of Twilight, *Edward is portrayed by Robert Pattinson and Bella by Kristen Stewart, both shown here.*

Lured by Twilight

THE FIRST BITE

Twilight's cover image is filled with meaning. Twilight, the time of day when light and dark meet, has been used as a magical time in literature dating back to the works of William Shakespeare. And the proffering of an apple, forbidden fruit, is inspired by the story of Adam and Eve in the Old Testament. It may seem surprising to find a combination of old literature and religion in a new-age love-fantasy story, but for this particular author, the combination makes perfect sense. In fact, Meyer used the English degree that she earned from BYU to insert many literary themes into her first novel, like the kind of forbidden love Shakespeare wrote about in *Romeo and Juliet*. Her Mormon upbringing provided the rest.

Twilight is the story of 17-year-old Isabella "Bella" Swan, who leaves her mother's home in Phoenix, Arizona, to live with her father in Forks, Washington. At the beginning of the story, her mother has recently remarried, and Bella unselfishly decides that living with her estranged father will allow her mother and her new stepfather to have a good start to their marriage. It is an extraordinary teenager who can make such a sacrifice, particularly since Bella knows that she will not enjoy her time with her father in the rainy, small town of Forks. But she is no ordinary teenager—as readers will come to find out soon enough.

Upon her arrival in Forks, Bella reveals herself to be an awkward teen, although one much admired by the male population of Forks High School. The most intriguing boy in school, Edward Cullen, is no exception, despite the fact that he is secretly a nearly 100-year-old vampire. Bella's first impression of Edward is that he hates her thoroughly. Because she does not understand why, she is immediately irritated and intrigued by his attitude. Their first encounter is hostile, and afterward, Edward disappears for a few days while Bella settles in to her new life in Forks. When he returns, Edward is suddenly more gregarious and engages Bella in conversation often.

The main characters' relationship continues to run hot and cold until the day Bella is nearly crushed by another student's car. When Edward saves her in a way that seems almost impossible, the intrigue ramps up as she tries to figure out how he could have done it, and indeed, why he would even bother, considering how changeable his attitude has been toward her. Even Edward's siblings seem agitated that he saved her life at all.

As the story progresses, Bella slowly uncovers the truth behind Edward and the other Cullens: They are a vampire coven, complete with adoptive mother and father vampires. Fortunately for Bella, Edward's coven is "vegetarian," meaning they subsist only on the blood of animals. Because humans are strictly off the menu, the coven enjoys a kind of freedom unknown to most vampires. Able to keep a home in one area for an extended period of time since there are no pesky bodies piling up, these vampires coexist among humans and conduct nearly human lives.

In this context, Edward and Bella are able to explore their romantic relationship, despite the fact that Bella's blood has a rare aroma that vampires, and Edward in particular, find hard to resist. The two seem supernaturally attracted to each other, but their love is strictly virtuous. Meyer's Mormon influence maintains an appropriate boundary between the two as she writes a romance that is passionate, but not physical. For Meyer, this restriction might be a matter of her upbringing, but in the context of the story, it is a practical matter. Vampire-human relations remain dangerous for both characters; physically dangerous for the human Bella, and heartbreaking for the immortal and love-smitten Edward. While many reviewers were flummoxed by the conflict between passion and chastity for the two lovers, for Meyer and her fans, this double-edged sword added necessary and believable tension.

The courtship of Bella and Edward is not without hindrances. When another group of vampires, the non-vegetarian sort, arrives on the scene, Bella is put in immediate danger. Here, in the last third of the story, a hungry vampire with keen tracking abilities is on Bella's tail. The novel breaks into a fast pace, accompanied with flashy cars and plane rides that seem tailor-made for translation to a movie screen. In the end, the vampires led by Edward triumph, and Bella is saved. The encounter also drives her supernatural and real-world lives together as her mother is introduced to her vampire boyfriend and his family.

THE REVIEWS ARE IN

Meyer's debut received mixed reviews from the critics. Don D'Ammassa complained that "the story goes on a bit too long and the climax doesn't really resolve the issues raised earlier, but it's not a bad book and should certainly find some enthusiastic fans."[1] Other reviewers also found fault with the book's pacing. Deborah Stevenson wrote, "The story moves slowly, spending an excessive amount of time on extended description and contemplation of Edward's physical beauty." Nevertheless, she tells potential readers that they may "find their appetites whetted by the risky, compelling romance."[2]

While the book was climbing the *New York Times* best-seller list, one reviewer wrote that "the book suffers at times from overearnest, amateurish writing. A little more 'showing' and a lot less 'telling' might have been a good thing, especially some pruning to eliminate the constant references to Edward's shattering beauty and Bella's undying love."[3] In *Vanity Fair*, James Wolcott griped that Bella's sighing over Edward was monotonous, "subjecting the reader to dumb-bunny clunkers such as this beaut: 'Edward stood in the halo of the porch light, looking like a male model in an advertisement for raincoats.'"[4] Yet Karen Cruze, writing for *Booklist*, was enthralled, calling *Twilight* "a unique tale" and promised that readers "will be eager to find out whether Edward will ultimately rescue, resist, or bite his love."[5]

Though the reviews were not all solidly positive, the story got a powerful response from readers. Little, Brown's original print run was unable to meet the demand of ravenous readers, who used their computers to connect to each other and spread the word about Meyer's vampire romance story. One reviewer got the mood of the fans exactly right: "Stephenie Meyer's swoony saga of vampires and young love—a Gothic romance for the age of Google—has grown from an OMG word-of-mouth phenomenon among teen girls to mass popularity among teens, and increasingly their mothers and teachers."[6]

HOME OF THE VAMPIRE

Forks, Washington, was a sleepy small town and the "Logging Capital of the World," according to a town sign, before more recently becoming the vampire capital of the country. In the 1980s and 1990s, Forks lost its timber business, many jobs, and even some residents. Named after the forks in the nearby Quillayute River and Bogachiel River and surrounded by spruce and fir trees, the town tried to rely on its nearby rain forest for tourism, but the influx of visitors was only seasonal. But salvation was coming, thanks to Meyer's debut novel. After *Twilight*, teenaged fans started arriving in the town in droves.

Marianne Ell and her daughter Annie drove 10 hours from Vancouver Island, Canada, to spend a little over a day in Forks. "It's completely worth it," Annie said. "This town is almost completely devoted to *Twilight*."[7] If you look at the town, and around the ever-increasing number of tourists who have come to take pictures with anything that says "Forks," you will find signs heralding businesses' support of the Twilight books—irresistible to the voracious Twilighter (as Meyer's fans call themselves). "Vampires Thrive in Forks" reads a sign above the visitor center in Forks. The sign for Weston Motors reads, "Welcome race fans and vampires."[8]

A note left for visitors taking the "Twilight Tour" is shown on September 5, 2008, at a house in Forks, Washington, portrayed as the home of teenage vampire Edward Cullen and his family.

"It's not hard to put [Twilighters] over the edge,"[9] said the manager of the Olympic Suites Inn. One of the bedrooms, "Bella's Suite," features red and black linens and fake, long-stemmed roses placed on the beds. It gets double the rate of a regular room and is advertised outside by a sign that reads, "Edward Cullen didn't sleep here!"[10]

Anna Vandenhole visited the town in 2008 with her son and his girlfriend. They got T-shirts and were looking for jewelry that Meyer herself helped to design, with charms inspired by the book. Vandenhole drove around town taking pictures of the local hospital, a two-story house, and an old red pickup truck. "How often have you ever taken a vacation to see a grocery store, a high school and a hospital?"[11] asked Janet Hughes of JT's Sweet Stuffs, a candy shop that has also gotten in on the Twilight trend by selling Edward Bites (chocolate-covered peppermint bark) and Bella Creams (mint buttercreams).

Mike Gurling, who runs the visitor center for the Forks Chamber of Commerce, encourages every Twilight tourist trap. Gurling came up with the idea of doing Twilight tours and posted information on the Chamber of Commerce Web site. Within hours, people were beginning to sign up. He encouraged Kim McIrvin to put a sign in her yard that reads, "Home of the Swans." McIrvin says that thousands of people have stopped by to snap pictures of her house ever since. "We think Bella's bedroom is up there," Gurling says, pointing to a second-floor window. "When you read the book, this is the perfect image of how you picture Bella's house to be."[12] A bed-and-breakfast was transformed into "the Cullen House." The front porch sign is now updated daily with fictional messages from Esme, the matriarch of the Cullen clan. Even the Forks Community Hospital administrator plays along. There is now a "Dr. Cullen Reserved Parking Only" sign in the parking lot.

For hungry Twilighters, Sully's Burgers offers the "Bellaburger," a hamburger topped with a ring of pineapple and a slice of Swiss cheese and served with a set of plastic vampire teeth. Manager Bruce Guckenberg says that in three months of beginning to offer the Bellaburger, Sully's sold 800 of them. And Sully's is not the only place to get a Twilight-themed meal. The local Subway sells a "Twilight

Special" sandwich, and other restaurants offer "Bellasagna" and "Bellaberry pie."

The fans take everything seriously, surprising many residents. "You would not believe how many people come in here expecting to see a vampire. Or a werewolf. I am not kidding,"[13] said the cashier at a local motel. Police Chief Mike Powell has even started to answer to his fictional counterpart's name, Charlie Swan. Sometimes, he even signs autographs as Charlie and poses for pictures with his squad car. "It's good for the town,"[14] Powell says, so he plays along.

But "some [residents] are taking to the attention like vampires exposed to sunlight,"[15] reported Marc Ramirez for the *Chicago Tribune*. And fans have noticed. "A few people who live there seemed like they were a little bit annoyed.

Did you know...

Forks is just one of many town offering Twilight-themed tours. Since no part of the *Twilight* movie was filmed in the town, tours are also taking place in the spots where the movie was actually filmed. The View Point Inn in Corbett, Oregon, was where the movie's prom-night scenes were filmed. They even have a Twilight-themed slumber party. Olympic National Park, 35 miles (56 kilometers) south of Forks, is the home of Kalaloch Lodge, which offers a two-night "Twilight Package." Beyond Boundaries Travel, based in Colorado, also has tours and events for Twilighters.

Maybe they like their peaceful town,"[16] said one teenage visitor. Residents confirm the sentiment. "Some people feel like, 'Why should we be known for vampires?'"[17] resident Linda Wells asked. Mark Brandmire, the assistant principal of Forks High School, agrees. Fans taking pictures of the school's Spartans sign, looking in the parking lot for Edward's silver Volvo, or wandering inside the school seeking the characters themselves, have besieged the school. "Our kids don't see the novelty," he said. "What part of 'fiction' don't you get?"[18] But the school may get some benefit. A group of fans called Twilighters for Forks have set up a Web site to raise money for the crumbling façade of Forks High School. The site has photos of Forks High current and past. One in particular, of students playing baseball in the 1920s, is said to be of Edward Cullen at bat during his first visit to Forks.

Meyer first visited the town in 2006, after *Twilight* had been published, and fell in love with it. "We have a little house we love to rent," she said. "There's bald eagles' nests in the backyard. For us, that's a big deal."[19] On her first visit, she met with a few fans for tours. The following year, the town organized a Stephenie Meyer Day on September 13, to coincide with Bella's birthday. By 2008, the event had grown so large that the day became a weekend. In 2009, the Chamber of Commerce started selling tickets and booking rooms in the spring for the September event. "I think it's every *Twilight* fan's dream come true to go to Forks and see where the book takes place,"[20] said one fan.

The front of Forks High School in Forks, Washington, as photographed on May 16, 2009. The town of Forks, long suffering from the decline of the timber industry, has been revitalized by a steady stream of visitors who are fans of the Twilight series, which is set in and around the area.

5

Over the Moon

ONCE IN A BLUE MOON

It is a rare thing for someone who had previously never written any fiction in her life to become an author. And it is far rarer for a first-time author to be showered with the kinds of riches that were offered to Meyer and to have her debut novel become an international best seller. But Meyer had done it effortlessly, and she had only just begun.

Immediately after finishing the manuscript for *Twilight*, Meyer began working on its sequel. While she was editing the first manuscript and sending out query letters, she found that she still had a lot more story to tell. Initially, the story took her way ahead to a future in which Bella and Edward were happily together, but as she was writing it, she realized that she had left out how the two had gotten there. She decided to go back and fill in the story that she had left out.

The sequel *New Moon* begins in the characters' senior year at Forks High School, with Bella and Edward firmly established as a couple, and Bella as practically a part of the Cullen family. Problems begin early in the novel, when on Bella's birthday, she accidentally cuts herself in front of her vampire family and their true natures arise. In an effort to save Bella from Jasper, who has the hardest time resisting human blood, Edward knocks Bella into a glass table that cuts her arm and worsens the situation. Practically all the vampires are hard-pressed to resist, except "dad" Carlisle, who stitches her up.

Edward decides that his relationship with Bella puts his paramour in too much danger. When the family abruptly leaves town, Bella is devastated. After months of hopelessness, she begins to put the pieces of her life together with a little help from Jacob Black of the Quileute Tribe, who is a longtime family friend. The fact that he is also in love with her is not lost on the reader, nor on Bella, although she hopes that they can just be friends. Bella also discovers that dangerous activities bring Edward's voice into her head, pleading her to stop. Because this mental connection is her only tie to him, Bella ramps up the danger factor in her activities, hoping Edward will come to her rescue. She gets two motorcycles that Jacob helps her fix up and learns to ride. She makes poor choices, and in a final act of desperation, goes cliff-diving by herself.

Because she is clairvoyant, Alice Cullen sees a vision of Bella's cliff dive and believes she has attempted suicide. She tells the other Cullens. Then a miscommunication over the phone leads Edward to believe Bella is actually dead, and he leaves for Italy to try to take his own life. Here, in the latter part of the book, the action picks up again, similar to the story arc in book one, as Bella and Alice race across continents to reach Edward and stop him in time.

Sales of *Twilight* were still picking up steam when *New Moon* was released just a year after the first book, but Twilighters were already spreading the word and helping to grow the fan base. And as Meyer realized that Bella and Edward's story would outgrow her three-book contract, Little, Brown happily amended to include a fourth book.

A SEQUEL WITH BITE

For *New Moon*, Little, Brown stepped up the initial print run to 100,000 copies. Shortly after the book was published in September 2006, the reviews came out. Once again, they were decidedly mixed. Calling the sequel "fabulous" in the opening line of her review for the *Journal of Adolescent & Adult Literacy*, Sandra Udall Crandall wrote that "Meyer's talent is such that her characters are realistically drawn and subtly nuanced. Even minor characters are so lifelike that they do not feel flat." She also praised Meyer's ability to draw in the reader and to describe locations that make reading to "almost like watching a movie."[1] Cindy Dobrez also wrote a favorable, though less enthusiastic, review for *Booklist*, noting that "romantics will miss Edward's presence, but the suspense created by a pack of werewolves bent on protecting

Bella from a vindictive vampire will keep them occupied until the lovers can be reunited." Her assessment was that "teens will relish this new adventure and hunger for more."[2] Much less enthusiasm came from a reviewer for *Publishers Weekly*, who declared that "fans of Meyer's debut novel, *Twilight*, may be disappointed in this second book . . . long stretches in the book may make readers feel as if they're treading water."[3]

Regardless of the reviews, the fans were thrilled by *New Moon*. Meyer, still getting used to the overwhelming fan response, quipped, "I say to all other authors: If you're not writing for teenage girls, you're missing out on a lot of love."[4] The second book introduced Jacob Black as a new love interest for Bella, one who, without Edward in the picture, seemed to be a realistic, even saner, choice given the circumstances into which Meyer wrote her characters. The fans became involved in the choice Bella had between the two and started wearing T-shirts that read "Team Edward" or "Team Jacob" everywhere they went. Since the rivalry continued into the third book in the series, the T-shirts had a fairly long shelf life.

New Moon remained on the *New York Times* best-seller list for a year, holding the top spot for 29 weeks. In 2009, Meyer's sequel sold approximately 19,800 books per week in Australia in the month of January; the previous record holder was Dan Brown's *The Da Vinci Code*, which sold 14,500 copies in the first month of its Australian release.

In the United States, *New Moon* continued to woo fans throughout 2006, just as *Twilight* had the year before. It also delivered on the promise of additional books in the series. As previously mentioned, Meyer realized that she had four books on her hands, rather than the three she had initially envisioned. She felt there was still much more to Bella and Edward's story, as well as a love triangle to negotiate. In 2006, Meyer was feverishly at work on the third book, with her eyes firmly set on resolving the series, at least from Bella's viewpoint, in a fourth book. At that time, Meyer was already thinking of continuing the story from Edward's perspective in a fifth book. It would be similar to the idea that Lori Joffs had when she started writing *Twilight* from Edward Cullen's viewpoint on FanFiction.net, only this time, it would be Meyer herself writing it, with her own particular insight into the characters and with the prose that her readers had already fallen in love with.

MUSICAL MUSE

Meyer's self-described obsessive writing had her working every day. Some days, she wrote just a page or so, but on other days, she was able to complete an entire chapter. Meyer was fueled by the characters in her imagination but also by the music that she blasted in her headphones as she wrote. She says, "Linkin Park was kind of the undercurrent of [*Twilight*] for me. I had *Hybrid Theory* and *Meteora* on a mix, and I just listened to them over and over again. They have a great rhythm for writing; aside from the tone of the song, the beat keeps you moving fast."[5] But Meyer was not a longtime music fan. She says, "Actually, growing up, I didn't listen to a ton. My parents were pretty strict. I only discovered music as an inspiration later in life."[6] She remarked in an interview with *Rolling Stone*: "They wanted to listen to everything before we listened to it, so basically we wound up listening to Lionel Richie and

Chicago."[7] She said college was a crash course in music education.

Music has since become an integral part of her writing method. "I listen to music always when I write," she told *Rolling Stone*. "When I hear music on the radio, I'm like 'Oh! That's a song for this character' or 'This one would so fit that character in this mood!'"[8] She said that the tunes come with the package. "The music is part of [my writing process]. I could not do without it."[9]

As she wrote *New Moon*, Meyer discovered the band Marjorie Fair. Their music, which she described as "soul-crushing, heart-breaking," perfectly fit Bella's depression after Edward disappears. She told *Rolling Stone* that the song "To the End of the World" was a perfect soundtrack for the scene in which Bella is looking for Edward in the woods at the start of the book. With *Eclipse*, the third book in the series, songs actually helped her to choreograph scenes. "Hysteria" by the band Muse was one of them. It inspired the scene in which Bella and Jacob kiss. "I can hear him in the beat as he's walking towards her. The scene is not everybody's favorite, but I certainly enjoy it."[10]

Did you know...

Meyer's use of rock and roll in her series has inspired musicians to create bands whose names are inspired by her books, including the Bella Cullen Project, the Twilighters, the Twilight Music Girls, and Midnight Sun.

Stephenie Meyer greets her ardent fans as she arrives at the Twilight *world premiere in Westwood, California, on November 17, 2008.*

6

Eclipsing Records

BLINDED BY *ECLIPSE*

In *Eclipse*, the third offering in the Twilight series, Meyer does a lot of backtracking to fill in the stories of the other major characters in the series. Readers find out how Jasper was turned into a vampire, why he is such a good fighter, and why being around humans is harder for him than the other vegetarian vampires. There is a backstory on Rosalie as well. As the coldest of the Cullens, Rosalie was a difficult character for Meyer to peg. "It took me a while to figure out what her thing was,"[1] Meyer said. But in *Eclipse*, readers might sympathize with Rosalie enough to understand how she and Bella could become so close in the fourth book. Meyer also delves into the Quileute lore and reveals how Jacob's wolf pack came to be, and why.

Like the first two books, there is trouble coming down the pike. Newborn vampires are turning up all over the place and wreaking havoc on society. Before the Italian Volturi family—sort of an Interpol for vampires—can stop them, the Cullens decide to deal with the problem themselves. In order to do it, however, the Cullens need to work with the werewolves, their mortal enemies. Fortunately, as the prize each side wants, Bella helps maintain their uneasy truce. And after all the planning and preparations, the main action finally comes at the end of the book, just like the previous stories, but not before the romantic complications ratchet up as Edward and Jacob vie for Bella's heart.

Despite the skyrocketing sales of her previous novels, Meyer was unsure how *Eclipse* would fare in the market. "It was the summer of *Harry Potter.* I thought I'd get steamrolled,"[2] she said. But *Eclipse* surpassed *Harry Potter and the Deathly Hollows*, the seventh and final book in the Harry Potter series, in sales, selling 150,000 copies on its first day alone.

Reviewing the novel for the *New York Times*, Liesl Schillinger wrote, "Bella sizzles with longing, agonizing over the Right Monster." Even when the war between the newborn vampires and the vampire-werewolf team ensues, Schillinger still thinks the reader would be occupied with other worries:

> Who could care, when what you really want to know is: Will Bella and Edward get married after they graduate from high school—given that once their vampire vows are solemnized, Edward will drain her blood and transform her into a

night-wandering predator? Or will Bella choose Jake, and raise a litter of dark-haired werepups?[3]

Cindy Dobrez in *Booklist* remarked: "In the third install-ment, decisions about college, marriage, and, oh yeah, immortality are pressing on heroine Bella Swan." While Dobrez was happy to see that Meyer's humor remains, she wondered where the action was. "The plot, which ultimately evolves into another war with evil vampires, unfolds at a leisurely pace."[4]

STRIKING A BALANCE

Meyer's books may be leisurely, but her own life had taken on a roller-coaster-like speed. Since she had first dreamed up the fictional couple, she had become a sensation among teen readers and their parents and an asset for Little, Brown. With one more book to go, and others on her mind, the author tried to make sense of her fame and still have a nor-mal life. It was proving to be difficult.

"I can't write with this kind of nightmare," Meyer told Megan Irwin in 2007, after coming off a couple of blows dealt by her fans. A year before, a review copy of *New Moon* had been leaked by a librarian, who posted spoilers from the book. Enraged fans who noticed that Edward was missing from most of the story lashed out at Meyer online for six months. Meyer felt like she was being attacked. "It was two days straight crying. I wouldn't have minded if [the librarian] went online and said she hated the book without posting the spoilers."[5]

Then, before *Eclipse* was published, Meyer lent a copy of the sequel to her sister-in-law, who then lent it to her sister (with Meyer's permission), but that sister passed it on to someone else. Eventually it landed in the hands of a

14-year-old fan, who made a copy for her friends. One of Meyer's loyal fans e-mailed to notify her of the leak. Meyer was horrified. But instead of getting upset, she set up a meeting with the girls and told them to keep mum. "I told them, if they don't talk, when *Eclipse* comes out, we'll have a party and I'll make them shirts that say 'I kept the *Eclipse* secret.'"[6]

The idolatry of her fans has been both good and bad for Meyer, who sometimes feels baffled by their love. She thinks that it is really all about the characters. About Bella, Meyer explained, "She's not a hero, and she doesn't know the difference between Prada and whatever else is out there. She's normal. And there aren't a lot of girls in literature that are normal."[7] Meyer admits to being that kind of girl. "If you're like I was, not in the popular crowd, a little clumsy, you have Bella to identify with."[8]

Many fans have responded to the characters as if they actually exist. "It's so sad that I've become so wrapped up and in love with a fictional character. It's like I really want an Edward in my life,"[9] one fan said. "They want them to be real," Meyer said of her readers and the characters she created. "I can't blame them. So do I."[10] The reason the characters feel so real is that Meyer herself wants them to be that way. "The sad part was, I'd be writing and it would be one o'clock in the morning, and then it would hit me: Edward's not real. But for the last six hours, he was. And then he would not be real again. Oh, it was heart-breaking."[11] And Meyer thinks that her passion translates. "I think people get that sense and how real it is to me. I think it helps make it real to other people."[12]

Dealing with her realistic characters was one thing, but her real fans demanded a different kind of attention. "I know some people might think it's kind of weird to be spending all this time and money just to meet an author for an hour," one fan said. "But for me it's really exciting. This is like meeting some big star to me, because I really admire Stephenie Meyer, and I admire that she could create these people and this whole amazing story."[13] And fans have been flocking to every event they can, spending a lot of money on transportation and lodging to ensure they see their favorite author as many times as they can. "They're not the largest group of fans out there," Meyer said, "but they seem to be the most fanatical." Meyer admitted to feeling uncomfortable with the adulation at first, but she has learned to deal with it. "I've gotten a little more confident; I'm better able to handle events,"[14] she said in 2007. And as much as they love her, she loves them back. She said, "It makes me want to adopt a teenage girl. . . . It's nice because I get to have a million teenage daughters."[15]

Meyer's love for her fans is clear every time she meets with them. After the *Eclipse* prom in 2007, Meyer showed up at an after party in her pajamas, her hair still done up for the prom. She slipped easily into the group of teen fans playing Twilight-inspired games like Twilight Cranium, which divides players into groups of humans, vampires, and werewolves. One fan started playing with her hair, and Meyer pulled another into her lap. Her fans think of her as a friend, someone they can rely on. One fan whispered happily to another that she knew Meyer would come to their party.

Even so, Meyer is still wary of her fame. In 2008, when *Time* asked her to respond to reader's questions, she said:

> When *Twilight* hit the *New York Times* bestseller list at number five, for me that was the pinnacle, that was the moment. I never thought I would be there. . . . I'm waiting for the rug to

be pulled out from under me. I have from day one because I'm kind of a pessimist. But it just keeps being huge.[16]

The result of becoming so big so fast has caused a lot of scheduling conflicts for Meyer, starting with that very first summer when she says she lost a lot of friends. "I'm still trying to find the right balance,"[17] she says. With the demands of book tours and other marketing events, Meyer's home life has become even more hectic, leaving her with less time for her husband and children. She told the *Phoenix New Times* that her children played a lot of video games because of her tight schedule, and that she felt badly about not giving them as much attention as she would have liked. In fact, her schedule became so demanding that in 2007 her husband quit his job to take care of the kids full time. The move helped to free up Meyer's time and allowed him to return to school to become an accountant. "Before she wrote an international bestseller, she was just a creative and intelligent woman. She's extremely blessed,"[18] Christiaan said. Her celebrity is a reality that she sometimes forgets

Did you know...

In 2007, Stephenie Meyer contributed to *Prom Nights from Hell*, an anthology of stories by some of today's most popular young adult authors, including Meg Cabot, Kim Harrison, Michele Jaffe, and Lauren Myracle. Meyer's contribution, "Hell on Earth," features a half angel named Gabe who comes to the rescue after warring biblical demons nearly destroy a prom.

while being a mom. "I'm a very normal, quiet person, and then I had to say, 'OK, I really am a writer now. I'm not just playing at this.'"[19] Following her breakout success, Meyer admitted to exhaustion. "The last 12 months seem like 10 years," she said. "My mom worries, 'Are you getting enough rest?'"[20]

But there is one caveat to her celebrity. "Writer fame is like 100 percent better than any other kind of fame," she said in 2007. "Unless I'm going to an event, no one will recognize me."[21] Besides, she still has her kids to think about. "I'm still a mom above all else. I'm glad that I still get to have my normal life. I get to have it all."[22]

VAMPIRE LOVE

In interviews, Meyer has admitted that those in the Mormon community have questioned her subject matter. In fact, writing about vampires surprised and embarrassed Meyer. She had never read Bram Stoker's novel *Dracula*, never watched the television series *Buffy the Vampire Slayer*, and never seen any horror movies because they are all rated R, and she will not see anything above a PG-13 rating. But the story she wrote, despite being about vampires, was one that appealed to a very different audience than the ones that might be enjoyed by the usual vampire enthusiast. Without sex or very much violence, the stories relied on a rather old-fashioned concept: romance.

"I get some pressure to put [in] a big sex scene," said Meyer. "But you can go anywhere for graphic sex. It's harder to find a romance where they dwell on the hand-holding."[23] The omission of sexual and violent elements is something many parents seem to appreciate. "It's a wonderful love story," librarian Carolyn Rancour said. "And it doesn't have sex. It's just so sweet. I think girls want to love and be loved."[24] Young fans agree. "[Edward is] what every girl wants her boyfriend to be. He's handsome beyond belief, he's polite, he's old-fashioned—he's a true gentleman,"[25] said one fan. Of the lack of sex, another fan commented, "They don't need to do that for a relationship to last. I think it sends a good message."[26]

Meyer notes, "I know a lot of kids who relate to my books because they don't drink and they are not sexually active. There are a ton of them but they don't get a lot of representation in literature or television or movies. Kids who are just good kids and follow the rules—they are out there and they don't get any playtime."[27] But Meyer did not write for those kids; she was writing for herself, and in so doing, found a population of teens who had the same feelings and values. "I didn't write *Twilight* thinking, 'Oh, I will appeal to 16 year olds with this.' I don't believe that you need to write down to teenagers."[28] As for her adult fans, Meyer is not sure of her appeal there either. "I don't know why they span the ages so well, but I find it comforting that a lot of thirtysomethings with kids, like myself, respond to them as

Did you know...

Susan Carpenter of the *Los Angeles Times* credits Meyer with creating a whole new genre. After the success of *Twilight*, other publishers, hoping to ride the wave of the new genre that Meyer popularized, started producing books centered on undead characters, including zombies and ghosts.

well—so I know that it's not just that I'm a 15-year-old on the inside!"[29]

While many found the phenomenon a bit of a head-scratcher, Orson Scott Card offered this explanation:

> In an era when much of the romance genre has been given over to soft porn, and dark fantasy is peopled with one-dimensional characters bent on grim violence, many readers have become hungry for pure romantic fantasy—lots of sexual tension, but as decorous as Jane Austen. Meyer . . . did not calculatedly reach for that audience. Instead, she wrote the story she believed in and cared about. . . . She's the real thing. Still, who'd have thought it? Today, Mr. Darcy [the main male character in Jane Austen's *Sense and Sensibility*] is a vampire.[30]

Prom-themed fans of author Stephenie Meyer attend the midnight release party for Breaking Dawn *at a Barnes & Noble in North Brunswick, New Jersey, on August 1, 2008.*

Breaking Molds

THE FINAL CHAPTER

Early in 2008, Little, Brown released a statement that the on-sale date of Meyer's final novel in the Twilight saga would be announced at midnight on February 7. Immediately, fans planned online countdown parties for the announcement. On the night of February 7, chats were filled with comments like, "Oh my God, 15 minutes to go to the announcement of the on-sale date,"[1] reported Andrew Smith, the associate publisher and vice president of marketing for Little, Brown Books for Young Readers. Little, Brown then made sure that book retailers had plenty of promotional materials to encourage preorders. When

Breaking Dawn was finally released at midnight on August 2, 2008, the one-day sales total was 1.3 million copies.

"We've got to get home and start reading,"[2] one fan said just minutes after getting her copy of *Breaking Dawn* at her local Borders just after the midnight release. But Jennifer Reese of *Entertainment Weekly* knew that this was probably not going to be a satisfying read. "Meyer takes her supernatural love story several steps too far,"[3] Reese said. Many other critics agreed.

Breaking Dawn begins with Bella and Edward's marriage and honeymoon, which one blogger claimed "read like a Harlequin romance."[4] The two go off to a remote island owned by the Cullens, Isle Esme. There they finally consummate their passion. For readers expecting the overly detailed descriptions that Bella was prone to before, there is disappointment. "Meyer writes about even furniture-wrecking sex with the decorum of a Victorian schoolmistress," said one reviewer.[5]

Immediately afterward, Bella becomes pregnant, and the rapid growth of her and Edward's offspring sets the book in a very different direction than the others. Jennifer Reese writes that "it's when Bella, suffering from morning sickness and gestating a vampire, starts vomiting 'a fountain' of blood, that Meyer jumps the shark."[6] At this point in the novel, Meyer stops telling the story from Bella's perspective and moves into Jacob's head for the middle section.

The couple returns to Forks, where Bella defends her pregnancy despite her growing weakness. Edward pleads for her to abort the baby, but Bella refuses. Jacob describes Bella's pregnancy in detail, including how she needs to rely on drinking blood through a straw to maintain the baby's strength as well as her own. When the child is finally born, kicking its way out and breaking Bella's bones in the process, Bella is saved from death by being turned into a vampire by Edward. A reviewer from the *Washington Post* wrote, "Reader, I hurled."[7]

After Bella's transformation, she takes over the narration again as the Cullens team up with other vampire friends from around the world to stave off the coming Volturi, who believe Bella and Edward have done the unthinkable: create a vampire child. Of course, the child is not really a vampire in the strictest sense, but the Volturi are determined to destroy the Cullens regardless. The transformed Bella and her newfound vampire super-abilities at last get a chance to save the day.

Meyer said that while she had no influence over the cover of the other three books in the series, she did have input on the final cover. For her, the chessboard signifies Bella's growth, moving from being a pawn in the story to being the most powerful player on the board, a fact borne out in the final moments of the book. But not everyone saw it that way. One reviewer remarked:

> The message that *Breaking Dawn* sends to girls everywhere is deplorable. This book doesn't seem to be about making difficult decisions and learning to dig deep inside yourself, find reservoirs of strength and lift yourself to great heights; rather, it seems to be about making inane, ridiculous decisions and never finding out what those decisions really cost. . . . Stupid, stupid Bella.[8]

Entertainment Weekly agreed: "As the masochistic teenage mother-to-be of a monster . . . [Bella] is not only hard to identify with but positively horrifying."[9]

But not all the reviews were bad. *Time* rated it an "A-,"[10] and the *Chicago Tribune* called it "a fun read."[11] As for the birth details that some found horrifying, other fans found

Justin Furstenfeld and Stephenie Meyer perform onstage at the **Breaking Dawn** *Concert Series in Times Square in New York City on August 1, 2008.*

realistic. "It makes a lot of sense within that context," wrote Laura Byrne-Cristiano on the fan site Twilight Lexicon. "Just thinking of any other number of vampire movies, it could have been a whole lot more gross."[12] But many fans were not so generous, and they were very vocal about it.

FANGED FANS

"It wasn't what I expected at all. It didn't seem to fit the world that I thought Stephenie Meyer created,"[13] said Katie Bludworth, a co-runner of the Bella Penombra fan site. "If all of the unhappy fans returned their books, it would send a message to Little, Brown and Stephenie Meyer. Don't let them profit from selling you badly-written, poorly-edited garbage,"[14] said one reader, according to *Publishers Weekly*. Some angry fans wondered if they should just burn their copies. Another declared, *"Breaking Dawn* will be hidden away in the darkest filthiest corner of my home."[15] The problem, according to reporter Sara Nelson of *Publishers Weekly*, was that Meyer became a friend to all of her readers. "And when a friend lets you down, well, you see what happens. . . . Still, one can understand how a teenager, deeply involved with an author's work and virtual personality, might want some kind of redress, or, like, explanation."[16] Many readers who posted comments on Amazon.com asked questions such as, "What was she thinking?"

Meyer responded. "To me, the story was realistic. Things do change, you do grow up, and the world changes,"[17] she said in response to a reader's question in *Time*. She told *Entertainment Weekly*:

> The negative reaction was so much more than I was expecting.
> . . . I knew that that was coming because I had read all of the

Did you know...

For the release of *Breaking Dawn*, Little, Brown sent Stephenie Meyer on a rocker-style music tour rather than a regular book tour. The *Breaking Dawn* concert series paired Meyer with Blue October's Justin Furstenfeld. In 2008, Furstenfeld told *Rolling Stone* that the pairing made perfect sense to him: "My songs are romantically dark, and her books are romantically dark."

expectations people had: "If this doesn't happen in the end, I'm going to burn the book!" I already knew the story so that didn't affect what happened, it just made me nervous for it to come out. But in the end I just had to say, "This is the way the story goes." . . . But I've been surprised at how hard it is to have people in some senses turn on you. That's weird for me. . . . It just got to the point where it was ruining my life to read these hate-filled, poisonous things about me. It was kind of horrifying. I really did have to learn to distance myself. I'm too negative of a person naturally, so I don't need any extra negativity. I'm not an optimist. One hundred people can tell you, "Oh, I love this, it's so great!" and one person can say, "I hate this, you're stupid." And that's the one I listen to because that's who I am. So I have to be careful.[18]

Little, Brown also released a statement about the reader response: "With a book that has been as eagerly anticipated as *Breaking Dawn*, it would be simply impossible to meet every reader's expectations. Stephenie Meyer's fans are tremendously passionate about her characters and emotionally invested in the lives she's created, so it's no surprise that they'd respond with equal passion and fervor."[19]

In the end, Meyer took it in stride. "Gosh, if I had to rely on giving people what they wanted, I would have had to write 40 billion different books, and even then, I wouldn't get it right."[20]

MORE BLOODLETTING

As if dealing with the venomous outpouring of disappointed fans was not enough for Meyer, when she returned from her book tour for *Breaking Dawn*, she learned that her manuscript of *Midnight Sun* had been leaked onto the Internet.

Earlier in 2008, Meyer had expressed her desire to continue with the Twilight characters after *Breaking Dawn*. "It's been such a big part of my life for the past five years, and it is an end of sorts, so it's kind of hard."[21] Meyer had been planning to write *Midnight Sun* since at least 2005; in early 2008, she posted the first chapter of the book on her Web site. This story, told from Edward's viewpoint, may have been an idea she got from Lori Joffs, the woman who created Twilight Lexicon. As previously mentioned, Joffs started writing a book from Edward's perspective after reading *Twilight*. Meyer's fans were already riled up. "If I don't finish it they'll come for me with torches and pitchforks. It's exciting. If I'd realized how much more fun it is to tell the story from a vampire point of view, I'd have started there."[22] Meyer put the book on hold while she went on the *Breaking Dawn* tour and concert series, but she was "looking forward to going home and getting back to writing."[23] It did not pan out.

"My partial draft of *Midnight Sun* was illegally posted on the Internet and has since been virally distributed without my knowledge or permission or the knowledge or permission of my publisher," Meyer wrote. "What happened was a huge violation of my rights as an author, not to mention me as a human being. I feel too sad about what has happened to continue working on *Midnight Sun*, and so it is on hold indefinitely."[24]

Meyer said that her lawyers actually wrote most of the statement, concerned that she would be too emotional. "I wrote about three single-spaced Word document pages of just real pain," she said. "I never felt any anger, actually. Just a lot of sadness. I mean it was a sucker punch—like someone came up behind you and just hammered you in the kidneys and you had no idea it was coming."[25]

Because Meyer knew how the leak happened and that there was no malice involved, she did not name names. She posted her draft on the Web site, she said, so that "my readers don't have to feel they have to make a sacrifice to stay honest."[26] Although she felt like she could not work on the manuscript then, she said that she would return to it someday:

> I do not feel alone with the manuscript. And I cannot write when I don't feel alone. So my goal is to go for, like, I don't know, two years without ever hearing the words *Midnight Sun*. And once I'm pretty sure that everyone's forgotten about it, I think I'll be able to get to the place where I'm alone with it again. Then I'll be able to sneak in and work on it again.[27]

SHIFTING INTO SCI-FI

In addition to *Breaking Dawn*, 2008 also saw the publication of Meyer's first adult novel, *The Host*. While sales of this book did not rival those of *Twilight*, it still did very well, and reviewers praised her development as a writer.

Charles de Lint, writing for *Fantasy & Science Fiction*, remarked:

> I've read somewhere that Meyer doesn't read [sci-fi] or horror, nor has she seen any genre films. While it begs the question as to why she writes in either genre, it does mean that she brings something different to the table. Her vampires and were-wolves—and her aliens in [*The Host*]—aren't different for the sake of being different (as a genre writer might attempt, staking out her own niche). They're different because she comes to them without the baggage of familiarity, approaching these tropes of our genre with a fresh eye that I find very engaging. For adult readers, *The Host* is definitely the place to start with her books.[28]

Meyer called the book "the first romantic triangle with only two bodies involved."[29] The story is about an alien named Wanderer who takes over the body of a young woman named Melanie, but she finds that Melanie is not so easily controlled. Wanderer decides to bide her time, waiting for Melanie to fail, but as the human resists and Wanderer has access to her mind and her emotions, she finds herself falling in love with her host's lover and caring about the people that Melanie loves. Further complications arise when another human falls in love with Wanderer while she is still in Melanie's body. *Publishers Weekly* called it a "tantalizing SF thriller" that "shines with romantic intrigue."[30] When it was released on May 6, 2008, Amazon.com named it a Best of the Month book. "For me I think *The Host* is my best-written work and also the most important story I've told so far,"[31] Meyer said in an exclusive interview for Amazon.com.

STAKE THROUGH THE HEART

After publishing four books in the Twilight series, an adult novel, and a piece in an anthology of stories for young readers, Meyer has proved to be prolific and popular. But despite astonishing sales, the critical response to her writing has been mediocre at best, and at times, downright biting.

Stephen King, one of the most successful and admired popular writers of recent decades, was asked in a January 2009 interview what he thought of the modern mainstream writers like J.K. Rowling and Meyer. "The real difference [between Meyer and Rowling] is that Jo Rowling is a terrific writer and Stephenie Meyer can't write worth a darn," he said. He went on to compare Meyer to Erle Stanley Gardner, the author of the popular Perry Mason mystery series of the 1930s: "He was a terrible writer, too, but he was very successful." King, however, said he understands the appeal for young girls. He believes the sensuality displayed between Bella and her vampire beau is "shorthand for all the feelings that they're not ready to deal with yet."[32] Meyer's fans were quick to defend her against criticism, saying that King had "sour grapes," despite the fact that King, with a decades-long career, is well entrenched in the publishing landscape, and that his success (over 350 million books sold) far surpasses Meyer's. Although King knows Meyer's work, she does not know his. "I just know I'm too much of a wuss for Stephen King's books," she said in 2007. "I'm waaay too chicken to read horror."[33]

King is not the only one comparing Meyer and Rowling. "Her story reminds one a little of J.K. Rowling's—Rowling wrote *Harry Potter and the Sorcerer's Stone* as an unemployed single mom while her baby daughter slept—and Meyer is quick to point out that her success is a direct result of the way Rowling changed the book industry," Lev Grossman wrote in *Time*. "But as artists, they couldn't be

Did you know...

Stephen King's *Salem's Lot* (1975) is considered one of the best vampire novels of all time, along with Anne Rice's *Interview with the Vampire* (1976), Richard Matheson's *I Am Legend* (1954), and the forerunner of all vampire novels, Bram Stoker's *Dracula* (1897). All four books have been made into movies. Stoker's *Dracula* and Matheson's *I Am Legend* have both been remade several times.

more different. Rowling pieces her books together meticulously, detail by detail. Meyer floods the page like a severed artery. She never uses a sentence when she can use a whole paragraph."[34]

Meyer is uncomfortable with the comparison between herself and the British author. She said, "I think [the comparisons] really come about because of the way our fans are so fanatic." She added, "Her fans obviously, but mine have a similar feel and I think some of that's thanks to her because people learned how to be fanatical through *Harry Potter*. Other than that though, she is a historically successful author."[35]

One blogger who was perplexed by Meyer's prose posted:

> What a load of grammatically incoherent, sexually repressed, Mormo-Victorian manipulation. I tried to pull my hair out after the first chapter, the syntax was so perplexing. . . . If this book had come to me from one of my ACT-prep students, I wouldn't have been so surprised. But from a thirty-something who has sold gazillions of copies of her novel and has been lauded as the American J.K. Rowling?! Pish posh, I say! Preposterous!!![36]

Meyer readily grants this. "I don't think I'm a writer; I think I'm a storyteller," she said. "The words aren't always perfect."[37]

Directed by F.W. Murnau, the German silent movie Nosferatu *(1922) is one of the earliest film portraits of a vampire. Shown here is actor Max Schreck as the evil Count Orlok.*

8

Her Own Brand of Vampire

REBIRTH OF THE VAMPIRE

"I don't read vampire stories or watch vampire movies, so I'm still learning," Meyer told the *Wall Street Journal* in July 2008. Meyer also admitted that she did little research into vampire lore as she wrote the Twilight saga. "I haven't even seen *Interview with the Vampire*," she said, speaking of the movie version of Anne Rice's famous book of the same name. "I change the channel really fast when horror movies come on," she continued. "I know the [traditional vampire] stories because everyone does, so I knew I was breaking the rules, but I didn't really think about it much until I started worrying. But vampire fans have been very open-minded."[1] Lizzie Skurnick of the *Chicago Tribune* agrees: "Her work may evoke the great icons of the supernatural landscape, as well as some teen titans (think Meg Cabot, crossed with Stephen King), but Meyer's delicious mix of life and afterlife is completely her own."[2]

What may have attracted Meyer to vampires is their physical beauty. She remarked: "If you look at the success of horror in general, you see creatures that are oozing, or they're dead, or in most cases really gross. Vampires are the only ones who are scary but still good-looking. It's double-edged. We're attracted to the darkness, but they have eternal youth and are very appealing."[3]

Every vampire storyteller has created their own rules and their own world for their characters. Within the vampire genre, there are many different variations of the vampire's

Did you know...

Vampires are so ingrained in popular culture that they have been defanged for consumption by children. The breakfast cereal Count Chocula debuted in 1971 and has been popular ever since. *Count Duckula*, an animated British television series, debuted in 1988. It featured a duck that was resurrected from the dead using ketchup instead of blood, which turned him into a vegetarian vampire. The children's book series that began with *Bunnicula*, first published in 1979, is about a bunny that sucks the juice out of vegetables; the latest book in the series was released in 2006.

world and the physical rules that govern the vampires, but some things remain the same. In all cases, the vampires are undead creatures. They have all had their blood transformed in some way to die and be reborn into their new vampire selves. They all require blood for survival. They all have some kind of special ability, and they all try to keep their true identities a secret from normal humans. But beyond those basic threads that connect them all, anything goes for the literary vampire.

KILLER CHARM

Beginning with John Polidori's 1819 story *The Vampyre*, vampires have been portrayed as elegant and charming. Polidori ushered in the modern vampire by making a break from previous vampire stories, in which the offending creature was simply a desiccated corpse. Polidori's main character, Lord Ruthven, is a British nobleman who preferred to feed on his own kind. In order to pass as human, Ruthven even becomes engaged, under the assumed identity of the Earl of Marsden. In Bram Stoker's *Dracula* (1897), the mysterious and charismatic Count Dracula seduces and entrances the two main female characters, Lucy and Mina, both of whom are the object of admiration of various other men in the story. Lucy and Mina are both drawn to Dracula, and after being bitten by him, succumb to his telepathic will. After Dracula turns Lucy into a vampire, the novel's male characters use Mina's connection with the vampire to find and destroy him.

The 1966–1971 ABC soap opera *Dark Shadows* introduced Barnabas Collins, a 200-year-old vampire who had been accidentally resurrected. In the twentieth century, he meets Maggie Evans, who Barnabas believed was the reincarnation of his long-dead love from a century past.

Christopher Lee was one of several actors who became famous for playing Count Dracula. Here, Lee is shown in Taste the Blood of Dracula *(1970), the fourth film in Hammer Film Productions' vampire series.*

Barnabas was portrayed as handsome and captivating, making the women in the series swoon, as well as female viewers, who found the actor playing Barnabas, Jonathan Frid, quite telegenic. Included among Frid's fans are director Tim Burton, singer Madonna, and actor Johnny

Depp. In an *Entertainment Weekly* article, Depp admitted, "When I was a kid, I wanted to be Barnabas. . . . He was super-mysterious."[4]

Meyer's Edward is just as mysterious, at least for the first part of *Twilight*. And like many other female characters, Bella is magnetically drawn to her vampire. Fortunately for Bella, her relationship with Edward is much more than the one usually found in most vampire literature—hunter versus prey.

IF LOOKS COULD KILL

Most vampires in literature have been beautiful—or at the very least, eternally young. They have the advantage of being frozen in time at their first bite. Modern movies perpetuate the image of the beautiful vampire, showing, for example, the characters from Anne Rice's *Interview with the Vampire* becoming more beautiful after being transformed to the undead. In Meyer's series, she explains that vampires' features become enhanced when they are transformed, so the already-very-beautiful Rosalie became a supermodel after her transformation. And already-handsome Edward became much more like a Greek god, so much so that Bella cannot stop commenting on his good looks. Since Polidori's writing, vampires have had pale skin. Prior to this, vampires were dark creatures, but Polidori's Lord Ruthven is pale and popular with the girls.

Vampires often have mesmerizing eyes. This feature helped some with transfixing their victims, but with others, it was just a physical trait. In *Interview with the Vampire*, Rice's narrator, Louis, has vivid green eyes, and Lestat, the vampire who transformed him, has grayish eyes that can absorb the colors around him, becoming brilliant blue and even violet. In Meyer's series, Edward and the other vegetarian vampires have bronze eyes when they have just fed, but their eyes become a darker, molten bronze when they are running on empty.

Some vampires even have interesting nails. Stoker's Count Dracula has nails that are long and shaped into a sharp point. When he seduces Mina and gets her to drink his blood, he draws his blood by cutting into his chest with his nails. In Anne Rice's books, Lestat and Louis both mention that their nails have a glassy quality, quite unlike the nails of humans. The emphasis on nails comes directly from early vampire hysteria, in which vampires were believed to grow new nails after death. Bodies that were exhumed were observed to see if the corpses had grown longer nails or if their human nails had fallen off to make way for their new vampire ones. Because the process of decomposition was not well understood in those times, natural decomposition caused many innocent corpses to be beheaded or have stakes driven through their supposedly undead hearts.

Woe to the human-turned-vampire who did not like their hairstyle before their transition. Meyer's vampires keep the same haircut forever. Anne Rice's vampires do as well, except that if they cut their hair after becoming a vampire, it grows right back to where it was before. In fact, in the days in which people believed in vampires, looking at the growth of hair on a corpse was also a way for vampire hunters to determine if a corpse had "turned."

TOO MUCH EXPOSURE

In the earliest depictions of vampires, they did not avoid sunlight and only go out by moonlight. Lord Ruthven, Dracula, and Sheridan Le Fanu's female vampire, Carmilla, from a novel of the same name, were all pale, elegant, and preferred the cloak of night, but none were bound to appear only in the shroud of darkness. While they had some weaknesses during the day, the sun was not a death sentence.

Today, however, most vampires avoid the sun. In Meyer's case, they avoid it not because it will kill them but because it turns their skin turns sparkly and brings them under scrutiny. The idea of sunlight being a natural enemy to vampires began with the 1922 film *Nosferatu*. (It is, in fact, the German film version of Stoker's *Dracula*, but it used a different name to avoid copyright infringement.) Directed by Friedrich Wilhelm Murnau, it is considered by many critics and fans to contain the scariest depiction of a vampire ever put to film—Count Orlok, a rat-eating, lowly vampire who hides from the sun as if light itself were a plague. The film's title comes from the Greek *nosophorus*, meaning "plague-carrier." Since plagues (such as the bubonic plague) terrorized Europe throughout its history, and vampirism was viewed as a plague itself, the name was quite appropriate. At the end of the film, Count Orlok is killed by the first rays of morning light. This innovation would become a common theme in vampire literature.

The idea of a vampire being killed by sunlight paralleled a religious view that sunlight represents good, while darkness or night represents evil. Vampires, as evil creatures, are unable to stand sunlight because of its inherent goodness and because it is a symbol of God. It is uncertain whether Murnau intended to create this parallel in the movie, but it became the predominant thinking after *Nosferatu*, and soon vampires all over fiction began shunning the sun.

But with a moral vampire, such as the ones depicted in Meyer's series, the good-versus-evil idea is explored in the conscience of the vampire itself. Meyer, like many authors, has been able to reject Murnau's sun-as-instrument-of-death convention by creating vampires who struggle with their own morality. When the struggle is internal, no external representations of good and evil are necessary. As a result, Meyer's vampires can happily go out in sunlight, at least when they are in the company of those in the know.

FANGED

None of the vampires in *Twilight* sport fangs. In their world, their teeth are strong as steel and razor sharp. On the fan site Twilight Lexicon, Meyer writes:

> My vampires do not have fangs. Their teeth are so sharp and strong that fangs are hardly necessary (they could bite through steel, if so inclined—a human neck is like butter, ha ha). The non-vegetarian vampires don't leave living victims (unless they are changing someone into a vampire); this isn't the neat-and-tidy, two-small-holes-in-the-neck kind of vampire attack that you see in other vampire mythologies.[5]

Of course, throughout literary history, vampires have sported fangs. Le Fanu's Carmilla had needle-like fangs that were barely visible. In more modern literature, vampires are often written with extended canines, the better to cut a jugular with. In some movies, vampire fangs retract and protrude as necessary. In the television series *Forever Knight*, the main character's fangs only protrude when his vampire nature is at the forefront. This is also the case with the vampires in the HBO series *True Blood*. In some versions of the myth, the fangs have tiny holes at their tips so that the vampires can suck blood directly through their teeth.

VEGGIE VAMPS

The Cullens are not the only vegetarian vampires in literature. Anne Rice developed that concept in the 1970s when she made her character Louis a moral vampire. Wanting to avoid biting and killing humans, Louis turned to rats. Other vegetarian vampires have appeared since then. In Adele Griffin's Vampire Island series for middle-grade readers, the main characters skip humans for food. In many other vampire stories where the vampire is either trying to come to terms with being a vampire while living in the human world or has a human love interest, the vampire is written to be sympathetic to humans and therefore only relies on blood from animals, in the case of the Cullens, or from blood banks, as actor Rick Springfield's character did in *Forever Knight*.

SPECIAL ABILITIES

Meyer describes her vampires as having supernatural abilities. In the Twilight world, vampires bring their strongest innate human traits with them after they become undead. Alice is able to see the future, a trait for which she was imprisoned in a mental institution during her human life. Edward can hear other people's thoughts, and Jasper is able to affect the emotions of the people around him. When Bella becomes a vampire, she finds herself able to project a protective shield around anyone, a mental ability that stemmed from her human life. She was protected from the probing abilities of other vampires. For example, Edward was unable to read her thoughts, and Jane, a member of the Volturi, was unable to create feelings of pain in her mind. In addition to these individual abilities, Meyer's vampires all have sharp hearing, acute vision, super strength, agility, speed, and gracefulness—all attributes that are not uncommon in vampire literature.

The only traditional supernatural vampire ability that Meyer does not give to her vampires is the ability to shapeshift. In many stories, vampires have been able to change into various other animals, most notably the vampire bat, or even a flock of bats, and in the case of Count Dracula, he could devolve into a mist at will in order to escape. Meyer saved her shape-shifting abilities for her werewolves.

VAMPIRE HYBRIDS

As it turns out, Renesmee, the half-human, half-vampire daughter of Edward and Bella, is not the only vampire hybrid in the genre. In *Breaking Dawn*, Meyer also brings in a South American vampire-human hybrid who saves Renesmee's life (along with all those who stand to protect her) by proving that vampire hybrids are not a threat to the secret world of vampires. Outside of the Twilight universe, some other vampire hybrids abound.

The *dhampir* of Balkan folklore was also a half human, born of a vampire father and human mother. However, in most descriptions, the dhampir looked a bit odd, with a snub nose, or sometimes no nose, and soft bones. In the comic book *Blade*, the dhampir was not created from a vampire father, but a vampire mother. In this case, his mother became a vampire while she was pregnant, which turned the child into a part vampire in the womb. Although most hybrids are the half-human, half-vampire sort, Adele Griffin's Vampire Island series features fruit-bat hybrid tweens who try to get rid of their pure vampire neighbor.

HOW TO KILL A VAMPIRE

Technically, since vampires are already dead, they cannot be killed. They can, however, be destroyed. In the Twilight series, the only way to destroy a vampire is to burn one, preferably after cutting them into a million pieces first, because, as vampires are quite resilient, they might be able to stop, drop, and roll, or to run into some nearby standing water to recover. And even when you do cut them up, they need to be burned quickly or their bits will piece back together by crawling back to each other.

Other literary and film vampire hunters had an arsenal of methods at their disposal, not the least of which was sunlight, as previously mentioned. A few of the standard methods include:

- Driving a stake through the heart. The idea of the stake through the heart came from early vampire hysteria in Europe. Vampires were believed to crawl out of their graves at night to prey on the living. The stakes were driven through the vampire's stomach or heart in a manner that literally pinned them to the ground so that they would not be able to crawl out. Eventually, this method developed into using a stake to drive through the heart because the heart was believed to be the location of the soul. You could use any kind of wood or metal stake to kill a vampire, but there is some preference for wood from the hawthorn, aspen, ash, or white thorn tree. This method of destruction was used in the novel *Dracula*, the 1985 movie *Fright Night*, Stephen King's vampire novel *Salem's Lot*, the film and television series *Buffy the Vampire Slayer*, and the Kiefer Sutherland teen-vampire movie *The Lost Boys*.

- Shooting them with a silver bullet. Because silver was considered to be pure, it was believed to work on most night pests like vampires and werewolves. In some cases the bullet needed to be blessed by a priest or the priest needed to be the one firing the bullet. In more modern versions, the bullet just needs to be pure silver. In the movie adaptation of the comic book *Blade*, Blade's silver bullets make vampires disintegrate.

- Pouring boiling water, boiling oil, or holy water on them. This would effectively kill any vampire.

- Cremating them. Meyer's Volturi carry around flame-throwers. Flame is useful for Meyer's creations and many other storied vampires. If facing an Anne Rice-type vampire, however, you also need to scatter the ashes, because blood from other vampires could turn them whole again.

- Beheading them. While cutting off the heads of vampires kills them in most versions, in Meyer's novels, the body can find the head and reconnect.

- Getting the head guy. In *The Lost Boys* and many other vampire tales, if the chief vampire is killed, so are all the subordinate vampires that he or she created.

In order to destroy the vampire, however, you might need to distract them first or weaken them in some way. They are super fast and super strong, so you need every tool you can get your hands on. A crucifix will drive some vampires back, but you have to be a believer in the Christian faith for that to work. Garlic, thought in many cultures to be a

Did you know...

The idea of the vampire being a compulsive counter inspired the *Sesame Street* character Count von Count, who likes to say, "I love to count things!" The count has been teaching preschool children basic mathematics since the show's second season.

healing medicine and a natural vitamin, is thought to have the properties of purification, much like silver. People sometimes hung garlic in doorways to prevent evil spirits from entering; doing so was a sure way to ward off vampires. You can also throw a pound of salt on the floor. Ancient vampires apparently were slaves to math and were forced to count things, such as every grain of salt that spilled on the ground. While they compulsively count, you have your chance to attack.

Of course, finding the right method to destroy a vampire depends on where you are in the world or where your vampire comes from. Each country seems to have a different method, depending on its myths, from the mild-seeming method of chaining the grave to the ground with wild roses (Bulgaria), to the quite gory method of boiling the head in vinegar (Crete).

With the popularity of vampire myths around the world, it is little wonder that Meyer happened upon a ready-made fan base for her romantic vampire story.

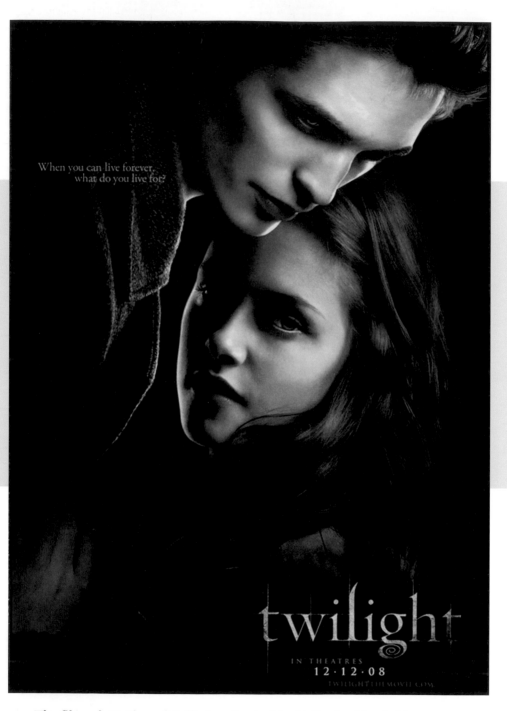

The film adaptation of Twilight, directed by Catherine Hardwicke, was an enormous commercial success upon its release in 2008. Shown here, the one-sheet film poster featuring Robert Pattinson and Kristen Stewart.

Beyond Books

LIGHTS, CAMERA, FICTION

"The Twilight series of novels has four of the top six spots on Amazon.com's best-seller list and the *Twilight* soundtrack is the nation's No. 1 selling CD, so it's not a real flying leap to figure out what's going to be the No. 1 movie in the country this weekend,"[1] proclaimed an article in the *Atlanta Journal-Constitution*.

That report in November 2008, just before the *Twilight* movie debuted, was the tipping point. Years of work on the movie deal and making the movie had passed, and everyone was waiting breathlessly to see what would happen that opening weekend—even Meyer. "There's so many people ready to say, 'Aha! See, we told you the movie was going to suck,'" she said. "There's that petty part of me that wants it to do really great so no one can say, 'All that buzz for nothing!'"[2] Meyer had no reason to worry. Fans lined up for days for the premiere.

"We drove from the Bay Area yesterday, got in line at midnight, slept out here, and stood all day in order to fulfill a dream to take a picture or get an autograph," said one adult fan. "And if that doesn't work out, it will still be worth it if we get to touch Kellan Lutz or Robert Pattinson."[3] Lutz and Pattinson, two stars of the movie, were unaware that so many fans were waiting, some for pictures and autographs, others with the demand: "Bite me!" Pattinson, who played Edward, said, "With every week, the anticipation seems to grow. People know my name, ambush me in public, try to figure out what hotel I'm staying at, ask me to bite them and want to touch my hair. It still feels surreal."[4] Kristen Stewart, who played Bella, added, "I've been to a lot of premieres, and none have ever been as big as this." She compared the fandom to Beatles-like hysteria and admitted, "I have never been moved enough to camp out for something."[5]

Even the film's director, Catherine Hardwicke, was elevated to star status. As she headed over to see who had turned up the day before the premiere, she was recognized by some of the Twilighters. "I ended up signing over 2,000 autographs. . . . It's like touring with the Grateful Dead."[6]

Paramount had originally optioned the movie but let the option expire in 2006. Summit Entertainment, a smaller studio, picked up the option, believing that an audience made up of primarily teen girls was a lock. Then they added some action scenes to entice the boys. The stunts, which involved putting Pattinson in a harness for racing up trees, were deemed "a cut above"[7] by one *Los Angeles Times* reviewer. Catherine Hardwicke became a fan of the books after reading them to prepare for directing the movie. Melissa Rosenberg wrote the screenplay, going through several drafts, including one in which Bella was made into a kind of action hero. In the end, she stuck closely to the book, even keeping lines like, "You're like my own personal brand of heroin." Rosenberg explained, "We've all had the experience of being that age and feeling that everything is life and death. . . . What's so wonderful about this story is that everything actually is life and death."[8] Hardwicke knew the stakes were high. "There's all this stuff online," she said before the movie's premiere. "People were making casting suggestions, and now they're doing their own trailers and posters."[9] The hardest thing for Hardwicke was figuring out what to leave out. "I wish I could make a six-hour movie," she said. "When you're a fan like I am, it's hard to let anything go."[10]

Even the casting was treacherous. Pattinson turned out to be a controversial choice for the role of Edward. At first, fans were unhappy with the choice and posted their anger on the Internet. "I apologized to him for ruining his life. . . . They just raked him over the coals,"[11] Meyer said. But he won the fans over, so much so that there was a Facebook web page just about his hair.

During production, Meyer and Pattinson clashed over how he would play Edward. "He'd sit there arguing with me, telling me I'm wrong about the character. He thinks Edward is a lot more depressed than I do. He thinks Edward is on the point of suicide," Meyer said. She tried to explain that Edward loved his family, Carlisle especially, and Pattinson challenged her. "Well, why does he like Carlisle so much? This man changed him into a vampire! What were you thinking?" It was not easy, as Meyer explains: "I was worried. . . . I was thinking, 'Oh my gosh, he's going to go in there and play Edward like Edward the emo. Noooooooooo. But he didn't! And it's exactly what I wanted to see. It was crazy, but he got it. It's on the screen and that's all that matters."[12] In a separate interview, Meyer noted, "His performance in my opinion is Oscar-worthy."[13]

Meyer was very involved with the movie's production and helped to ensure that it was rated PG-13, particularly since, as a Mormon, she had never seen an R-rated film. She watched the rough cut with friends, thinking she would need the moral support, and had a notepad ready. In the end, she only had minor notes. She wanted the meadow scene to be longer and asked that the filmmakers add a scene with Jacob at the prom. But there were a lot of things she loved. "I'd be watching what Catherine did with a scene, and I'd think to myself, 'Why didn't I think of that?'"[14] She said, "I could have watched it all night in a loop"[15] and added that she thought the ending was fantastic, too. "Now I've got them. They have to go on [with more movies], don't they?"[16] The author even makes an appearance about halfway through the movie, when Bella and her father are at a diner. "That's the only part I'm never going to watch,"[17] she said.

The fan response was terrific. "I went in expecting it to be crap and completely ruin my idea of the books," a 31-year-old moviegoer said. "And it completely amazed me."[18] The woman saw the movie three times that opening weekend. Some male viewers were disappointed. "We're hoping to see at least a couple of teenage girls get their heads cut off," one said. "I love vampire movies. . . . But this one was one of the worst!"[19] Another man, with the opposite opinion, proposed to his girlfriend during the credits.

Stephenie and Christiaan Meyer arrive at the premiere of Twilight *on November 17, 2008 in Westwood, California. The couple have been married since 1994.*

Movie reviewers were not quite as enthusiastic. "The term 'meh' was added to the dictionary this week, and just in time," Matt Pais of the *Chicago Tribune* remarked. He also called the effects "cheap-looking."[20] Even Meyer agreed with that; she thought the effect of Edward in the meadow had him looking more sweaty than sparkly. In the *Wall Street Journal*, Joe Morgenstern wrote, "All 13-year-old female readers of this newspaper: Run, do not walk, to the nearest multiplex playing 'Twilight.'" Then he added, "Others needn't run. Or walk."[21]

In November 2009, the first sequel in the Twilight Film series, *New Moon*, debuted in theaters. Although it met with mixed reviews, the movie earned nearly $143 million in its opening weekend alone.

SIREN SONG

In September 2008, Stephenie Meyer put her storytelling prowess to work on something entirely different: a music video. The band Jack's Mannequin asked if she would contribute to the making of their music video for "The

> ## Did you know...
>
> *Twilight* made Hardwicke the highest-grossing female movie director of all time (the film grossed $35 million on opening day), but by the end of the year, after heated negotiations, Summit Entertainment decided on director Chris Weitz for the sequel, *New Moon*. Another director, David Slade, was tapped to film the third movie, *Eclipse*.

Resolution," a single off their album *The Glass Passenger.* In writing the video, Meyer relied on her love for fantasy and created a situation in which a mermaid is stalking the lead singer, Andrew McMahon. "It's sort of a fable," she said. "This mermaid doesn't take no for an answer. The more he tries to get away from her, the greater lengths she goes to be able to reach him."[22] McMahon added, "Essentially, the tide is rising and keeps following us."[23]

To prepare, Meyer gathered a group of her friends for a music-video screening and went over all the videos that she loved. The screening included OK Go's "Here It Goes Again," Brand New's "Sic Transit Gloria . . . Glory Fades," and My Chemical Romance's "Helena," which Meyer said was her favorite video of all time because of the use of interpretative dance. As for directing, Meyer wisely turned the reins over to someone else. "I don't know much about directing," she said. "It's a total fluke. I'm just doing it [writing the video] because it's fun and an experience I never had, and I didn't want to turn it down. I certainly wouldn't say I'm going to be a music director now! I don't even know how to work the camera, and they won't let me."[24] Meyer added that she was more of a creative consultant and that she was just there to be sure the vision of the video worked.

The video was shot in one day in Malibu, California, where the video crew could get shots of the ocean, the desert, and a mountaintop to get the sense of travel without the travel. After 14 hours of shooting, Meyer, who was treated like royalty with a person holding an umbrella for her in the sun, was worried about getting it all done by the end of the day. But like all Meyer's stories, this one had a satisfying finish.

THE LAST DROP

It is unclear whether the Jack's Mannequin video had an impact on what Meyer wanted to work on next, or whether she took a story that she was already kicking around and injected it into the music video, but in 2008, Meyer was setting her sights on working on a story that involved mermaids, though she was reluctant to make it definite.

"I'm a little more hesitant to say what I'm working on, though, because people for some reason seem to take that as some kind of contract: 'You said you were working on this so now you have betrayed my trust by not doing it!' But I'm thinking I'm actually leaning towards the mermaids' story right now."[25] Though Meyer says she will not use the word "mermaids" in the story, instead she calls the characters "sirens."

Regardless, Meyer is sticking with fantasy despite the fact that prior to writing *Twilight* she was not a fan of the genre. Still, Meyer does not follow the usual trappings of the fantasy genre: Her vampires hardly bite and her aliens do not shoot ray guns. She seems more interested in the relationships of people within the fantastic situations she dreams up. "That's what I like about science fiction," she said. "It's the same thing I like about Shakespeare. You take people, put them in a situation that can't possibly happen, and they act the way you would act. It's about being human."[26]

So what is next for Meyer? "I have a novel started that would be a Mormon comedy romance," she said. "I do wonder what it would be like, because I have these girls who will read anything I write, so I know they'll read it, and I can't imagine what their reaction would be. And what parents will think about their kids reading stuff that has quite a lot of Mormon doctrine in it."[27]

Meyer encourages all writers to do as she did and figure out what they really want to say. "I didn't plan to start a new career when I did this, and it took a lot of courage to send out those query letters. I sent 15, and I got nine rejection letters, five no responses and one person who wanted to see me. If it's something you enjoy, put the determination and will behind it and see what happens,"[28] she said in answer to a reader's question on *Time*'s Web site. She added:

> If you love to write, then write. Don't let your goal be having a novel published, let your goal be enjoying your stories. However, if you finish your story and you want to share it, be brave about it. Don't doubt your story's appeal. If you are a good reader, and you know what is interesting, and your story is interesting to you, then trust that. If I would have realized that the stories in my head would be as intriguing to others as they were to me, I would probably have started writing sooner.[29]

CHRONOLOGY

1973 Stephenie Morgan is born in Connecticut on December 24.

1977 The Morgan family moves to Arizona.

1991 She enrolls at Brigham Young University in Utah.

1994 She meets Christiaan "Pancho" Meyer during summer break from college; the couple marry in December.

1995 Meyer graduates from Brigham Young University with a B.A. in literature.

1997 The Meyers' first son, Gabe, is born.

2000 The Meyers have a second son, named Seth.

2002 Eli, the Meyers' third son, is born.

2003 On June 2, Meyer has a dream about a vampire; she begins to write *Twilight*; in the fall, she gets an agent; in December, she accepts a three-book deal from Little, Brown.

2005 *Twilight* is published.

2006 *New Moon* is published.

2007 The Eclipse Prom is held at Arizona State University in May; in August, *Eclipse* is published; the anthology *Prom Nights from Hell* is published.

2008 *The Host* is published in April; *Breaking Dawn* is published in August; the *Twilight* movie debuts in November.

2009 *New Moon* is released in theaters.

2010 *Eclipse* is released in theaters.

NOTES

Chapter 1

1 Megan Irwin. "Charmed." *Phoenix New Times*, July 12, 2007. http://www.phoenixnewtimes.com/2007-07-12/news/charmed.

2 "Authors: Interviews: Stephenie Meyer." Young Adult (& Kid's) Books Central, September 2006. http://www.yabookscentral.com/cfusion/index.cfm?fuseAction=authors.interview&author_id=1564&interview_id=121.

3 Alyssa Braithwaite, "Fed: Is US Author Stephenie Meyer the New JK Rowling?" AAP General News Wire, July 25, 2008.

4 P.J. Standlee. "Stephenie Meyer, J.S. Lewis and More Young Adult Authors Fight Cancer with Project Book Babe." *Phoenix New Times*, April 7, 2009. http://blogs.phoenixnewtimes.com/uponsun/2009/04/stephenie_meyer_js_lewis_and_m.php.

5 Susan Carpenter, "Web Gave 'Twilight' Fresh Blood; Stephenie Meyer Grew Her Books' Readership with a Constant, Open, Grateful and Helpful Online Presence," *Los Angeles Times* (November 29, 2008): p. E1.

6 Ibid.

7 Nat Ives, "Making Release of 'Breaking Dawn' One for the Books," *Advertising Age* (August 11, 2008): p. 7.

8 Heather Green, "Harry Potter with Fangs—and a Social Network," *BusinessWeek* (August 11, 2008): p. 44.

9 Ibid.

10 Twilight Lexicon. "Email Subject: Stephenie Meyer Biography." E-mail with Tracey Baptiste, March 5, 2009.

11 Stephenie Meyer. "March 27, 2009." The Official Website of Stephenie Meyer. http://stepheniemeyer.com.

12 "Home Page." TwilightMOMS. http://www.twilightmoms.com.

13 Green, "Harry Potter with Fangs—and a Social Network," p. 44.

14 "Walmart to Add 'Twilight Shops' in All Stores in March with Arrival of Movie DVD." PR Newswire. http://news.prnewswire.com/DisplayReleaseContent.aspx?ACCT=104&STORY=/www/story/02-12-2009/0004971094&EDATE.

15 Donna Freitas, "The Next Dead Thing," *Publishers Weekly* (November 17, 2008): p. 23.

Chapter 2

1 Cynthia Leitich Smith. "Author Interview: Stephenie Meyer on Twilight." Cynsations, March 27, 2006. http://cynthialeitichsmith.blogspot.com/2006/03/author-interview-stephenie-meyer-on.html.

2 Stephenie Meyer. "Unofficial Bio." The Official Website of Stephenie Meyer. http://stepheniemeyer.com/bio_unofficial.html.

3 Ibid.

4 Jamie Rose. "The 'Twilight' Zone: Valley Author Thrust into Stardom." *Arizona Republic*, November 21, 2008. http://www.azcentral.com/arizonarepublic/news/articles/2008/11/21/20081121twilightbuzz21a1.html.

5 Meyer, "Unofficial Bio."

6 Ibid.

7 Ibid.

8 Irwin, "Charmed."

9 Ibid.

10 Ibid.

11 Ibid.

12 Meyer, "Unofficial Bio."

13 Irwin, "Charmed."

14 Ibid.

15 Richard N. Ostling and Joan K. Ostling, *Mormon America*. New York: HarperCollins, 2007, p. 185.

16 "10 Questions for Stephenie Meyer," *Time*, August 21, 2008. http://www.time.com/time/magazine/article/0,9171,1834663,00.html.

17 Stephenie Meyer, *Twilight*. New York: Little, Brown, 2005, p. 308.

18 Stephenie Meyer, *New Moon*. New York: Little, Brown, 2006, p. 36.

19 Meyer, *New Moon*, pp. 36–37.

20 Stephenie Meyer, *Eclipse*. New York: Little, Brown, 2007, p. 453.

21 Ibid.

22 Stephenie Meyer, *Breaking Dawn*. New York: Little, Brown, 2008, p. 652.

23 Meyer, *Eclipse*, p. 598.

24 Irwin, "Charmed."

25 "10 Questions for Stephenie Meyer."

Chapter 3

1 Irwin, "Charmed."

2 Stephenie Meyer. "The Story Behind *Twilight*." The Official Website of Stephenie Meyer. http://stepheniemeyer.com/twilight.html.

3 Jeffrey A. Trachtenberg, "Booksellers Find Life After Harry in a Vampire Novel," *Wall Street Journal* (August 10, 2007): p. B1.

4 Erica Futterman. "*Twilight* Author Stephenie Meyer on Her Upcoming Movie and Mermaid Dreams." *Rolling Stone*, August 8, 2008. http://www.rollingstone.com/news/story/22493653/dawn_of_the_undead.

5 Irwin, "Charmed."

6 Trachtenberg, "Booksellers Find Life After Harry in a Vampire Novel," p. B1.

7 Meyer, "The Story Behind *Twilight*."

8 Lev Grossman. "Stephenie Meyer: A New J.K. Rowling?" *Time*, April 24, 2008. http://www.time.com/time/magazine/article/0,9171,1734838,00.html.

9 Cecelia Goodnow, "Debut Writer Shines with 'Twilight.'" *Seattle Post-Intelligencer* (October 8, 2005): p. E1.

10 Meyer, "The Story Behind *Twilight*."

11 Rachel Deahl, "Little, Brown Has Big Plans for Meyer." *Publishers Weekly* 254 (July 23, 2007): p. 19.

12 Irwin, "Charmed."

13 Futterman, "*Twilight* Author Stephenie Meyer on Her Upcoming Movie and Mermaid Dreams."

14 Goodnow, "Debut Writer Shines with 'Twilight,'" p. E1.

Chapter 4

1 Don D'Ammassa, "Twilight," *Chronicle* (December 2005/January 2006): p. 31.

2 Deborah Stevenson, "Twilight," *Bulletin of the Center for Children's Books* (December 2005): p. 195.

3 Elizabeth Spires. "'Enthusiasm,' by Polly Shulman and 'Twilight,' by Stephenie Meyer." *New York Times*, February 12, 2006. http://www.nytimes.com/2006/02/12/books/review/12 spires.html.

4 James Wolcott. "The Twilight Zone." *Vanity Fair*, December 2008. http://www.vanityfair.com/culture/features/2008/12/twilight200812?printable=true&currentPage=all.

5 Karen Cruze, "Twilight," *Booklist* (March 1, 2006): p. 105.

6 Phil Kloer, "First Look: 'Twilight': Vampires, Romance and Hair—Oh My!" *Atlanta Journal-Constitution* (November 20, 2008): p. E1.

7 Susan Carpenter, "Column One; Your Next Stop: The 'Twilight' Zone; Thousands of Fans Have Visited the Town Where the Vampire Novels Are Set. The Town Is Drinking It Up," *Los Angeles Times* (November 15, 2008): p. A1.

8 Marc Ramirez, "Vampire Series Brings Washington Town Back from the Dead," *Chicago Tribune* (August 17, 2008): p. 9.

9 Carpenter, "Column One," p. A1.

10 Ibid.

11 Ibid.

12 Ramirez, "Vampire Series Brings Washington Town Back from the Dead," p. 9.

13 Ibid.

14 Carpenter, "Column One," p. A1.

15 Ramirez, "Vampire Series Brings Washington Town Back from the Dead," p. 9.

16 Ibid.

17 Ibid.

18 Carpenter, "Column One," p. A1.

19 Cecelia Goodnow, "A Bite of Romance; Stephenie Meyer's Forks-based Saga of Teen Vampire Love Is Now a Global Hit," *Seattle Post-Intelligencer* (August 7, 2007): p. C1.

20 Cecelia Goodnow, "A Vampire Romance; 'Twilight' Author's Teen Fans Have True Love Flowing Through Their Veins," *Seattle Post-Intelligencer* (June 29, 2006): p. C1.

Chapter 5

1 Sandra Udall Crandall, "New Moon," *Journal of Adolescent & Adult Literacy* (September 2007): p. 79.

2 Cindy Dobrez, "New Moon," *Booklist* 102 (July 2006): p. 51.

3 "New Moon," *Publishers Weekly* (July 17, 2006): p. 159.

4 Gregory Kirschling, "Stephenie Meyer's 'Twilight' Zone," *Entertainment Weekly* (August 10, 2007): p. 74.

5 Erica Futterman. "Why Stephenie Meyer Gave Her Vampire Book (and Soon-to-Be Film) Series a

Rock & Roll Soundtrack of Muse, Linkin Park, Blue October and More." *Rolling Stone*. August 8, 2008. http://www.rollingstone.com/news/story/22493653/dawn_of_the_undead.

6 "10 Questions for Stephenie Meyer."

7 Futterman, "Why Stephenie Meyer Gave Her Vampire Book (and Soon-to-Be Film) Series a Rock & Roll Soundtrack of Muse, Linkin Park, Blue October and More."

8 Ibid.

9 Denise Martin. "'Twilight': Stephenie Meyer Lets Her Inner Fangirl Loose at the 'Breaking Dawn' Concert Series." *Los Angeles Times*, August 8, 2008. http://latimesblogs.latimes.com/herocomplex/2008/08/twilight-stephe.html.

10 Futterman, "Why Stephenie Meyer Gave Her Vampire Book (and Soon-to-Be Film) Series a Rock & Roll Soundtrack of Muse, Linkin Park, Blue October and More."

Chapter 6

1 "10 Questions for Stephenie Meyer." http://www.time.com/time/magazine/article/0,9171,1834663,00.html.

2 Futterman, "*Twilight* Author Stephenie Meyer on Her Upcoming Movie and Mermaid Dreams."

3 Liesl Schillinger, "Children's Books/Young Adult, Eclipse." *New York Times Book Review* (August 12, 2007): p. 19.

4 Cindy Dobrez, "Eclipse," *Booklist* 104 (September 15, 2007): p. 74.

5 Irwin, "Charmed."

6 Ibid.

7 Kirschling, "Stephenie Meyer's 'Twilight' Zone," p. 74.

8 Bob Meadows and Kari Lydersen, "Stephenie Meyer Written in Blood," *People* (September 8, 2008): p. 90.

9 Ibid.

10 Goodnow, "A Bite of Romance," p. C1.

11 Futterman, "*Twilight* Author Stephenie Meyer on Her Upcoming Movie and Mermaid Dreams."

12 Braithwaite, "Fed: Is US Author Stephenie Meyer the New JK Rowling?"

13 Goodnow, "A Vampire Romance," p. C1.

14 Ibid.

15 Irwin, "Charmed."

16 "10 Questions for Stephenie Meyer."

17 Smith, "Author Interview."

18 Irwin, "Charmed."

19 Futterman, "*Twilight* Author Stephenie Meyer on Her Upcoming Movie and Mermaid Dreams."

20 Meadows and Lydersen, "Stephenie Meyer," p. 90.

21 Irwin, "Charmed."

22 Goodnow, "A Bite of Romance," p. C1.

23 Grossman, "Stephenie Meyer."

24 Goodnow, "A Vampire Romance," p. C1.

25 Ibid.

26 Ibid.

27 Damian Whitworth. "Harry Who? Meet the New J.K. Rowling." London *Times*, May 13, 2008.

http://entertainment.timesonline.
co.uk/tol/arts_and_entertainment/
books/article3917660.ece.

28 Kirschling, "Stephenie Meyer's
'Twilight' Zone," p. 74.

29 "10 Questions for Stephenie
Meyer."

30 Orson Scott Card. "Stephenie
Meyer," *Time*, April 30, 2008.
http://www.time.com/time/
specials/2007/time100/article/
0,28804,1733748_1733752_
1736282,00.html.

Chapter 7

1 Ives, "Making Release of 'Breaking
Dawn' One for the Books," p. 7.

2 Jennifer Reese, "Breaking Dawn,"
Entertainment Weekly (August 15,
2008): p. 68.

3 Ibid.

4 "Stephenie Meyer." Fantasy
Literature. http://www.fantasy
literature.net/meyerstephenie.html.

5 Reese, "Breaking Dawn," p. 68.

6 Ibid.

7 Elizabeth Hand, "Love Bites,"
Washington Post (August 10, 2008):
p. BW07.

8 "Stephenie Meyer."

9 Reese, "Breaking Dawn," p. 68.

10 "The Short List of Things to Do,"
Time, August 8, 2008, http://www.
time.com/time/specials/2007/
article/0,28804,1623143_1830841_
1830843,00.html.

11 Mary Harris Russell, "'Breaking
Dawn,' by Stephenie Meyer,"
Chicago Tribune, August 9, 2008,
http://www.chicagotribune.com/
entertainment/books/chi-stephenie-
meyer-09aug09,0,6606840.story.

12 Kate Ward, "Out for Blood,
'Twilight' Fans Bite Back at the
New Book," *Entertainment Weekly*
(August 15, 2008): p. 8.

13 Ibid.

14 Sara Nelson, "Breaking Trust?"
Publishers Weekly 255 (August 11,
2008): p. 5.

15 Ibid.

16 Ibid.

17 "10 Questions for Stephenie
Meyer."

18 Karen Valby. "Stephenie Meyer
Talks 'Twilight.'" EW.com,
November 5, 2008. http://
www.ew.com/ew/article/
0,,20234559_20234567_
20238527,00.html.

19 Ward, "Out for Blood, 'Twilight'
Fans Bite Back at the New Book,"
p. 8.

20 Denise Martin, "Meyer Watches as
Her Vampires Rise," *Los Angeles
Times* (November 21, 2008):
p. E12.

21 Braithwaite, "Fed: Is US Author
Stephenie Meyer the New JK
Rowling?"

22 Jeffrey A. Trachtenberg, "Author
Q&A Stephenie Meyer: In the
'Twilight' Zone. The Best-selling
Author Talks About Romance,
Fantasy and her (Vampire)
Stake in the Book World," *Wall
Street Journal*, July 31, 2008,
http://online.wsj.com/article/
SB121727805625790873.html.

23 Ibid.

24 Stephenie Meyer. "*Midnight Sun:
Edward's Version of Twilight.*"
The Official Website of Stephanie
Meyer. http://stepheniemeyer.com/
midnightsun.html.

25. Valby, "Stephenie Meyer Talks 'Twilight.'"

26 Meyer, "*Midnight Sun.*"

27 Valby, "Stephenie Meyer Talks 'Twilight.'"

28 Charles de Lint, "The Host," *Fantasy & Science Fiction* (December 2008): p. 38.

29 Goodnow, "A Bite of Romance," p. C1.

30 "Fiction Reviews." *Publishers Weekly*, March 31, 2008. http://www.publishersweekly.com/article/CA6545564.html?q= fiction+reviews+3%2F31%2F 2008,

31 "Amazon Exclusive: Stephenie Meyer Talks About *The Host.*" Amazon.com. http://www.amazon.com/Host-Novel-Stephenie-Meyer/dp/0316068047.

32 Lorrie Lynch. "Exclusive: Stephen King on J.K. Rowling, Stephenie Meyer." *USA Weekend*, February 2, 2009. http://blogs.usaweekend.com/whos_news/2009/02/exclusive-steph.html.

33 Kirschling, "Stephenie Meyer's 'Twilight' Zone," p. 74.

34 Grossman, "Stephenie Meyer."

35 Braithwaite, "Fed: Is US Author Stephenie Meyer the New JK Rowling?"

36 Boyd Vogeler. "Stephenie Meyer Sucks Blood Out of Literature." Boyd Where Prohibited. http://ebv.blogspot.com/2008/05/stephenie-meyer-sucks-blood-out-of.html.

37 Grossman, "Stephenie Meyer."

Chapter 8

1 Irwin, "Charmed."

2 Lizzie Skurnick, "A Killer Series; In Her 'Twilight' Novels, Stephenie Meyer Offers Her Own Original Take on Life—and the Afterlife," *Chicago Tribune* (August 2, 2008): p. 4.

3 Trachtenberg, "Author Q&A Stephenie Meyer."

4 "Johnny Depp: Cutting Loose in 'Sweeny Todd.'" *Entertainment Weekly*, November 9, 2007. http://www.ew.com/ew/article/0,,20155516_20155530_20156283_5,00.html.

5 "Conversations with Stephenie Meyer." Twilight Lexicon Blog. http://www.twilightlexiconblog.com/?p=34.

Chapter 9

1 Kloer, "First Look," p. E1.

2 Karen Valby, "No. 5: Stephenie Meyer," *Entertainment Weekly* (November 21, 2008): p. 44.

3 Carrie Bell, "The 'Twilight' Premiere: Hysteria and Happy Campers," *Entertainment Weekly* (November 28, 2008): p .9.

4 Ibid.

5 Ibid.

6 Ibid.

7 Susan King, "David Strick's Hollywood Backlot; 'Twilight' Stunts Are a Cut Above," *Los Angeles Times* (November 20, 2008): p. E3.

8 Terrence Rafferty, "Love and Pain and the Teenage Vampire Thing,"

New York Times (November 2, 2008): p. MT6.

9 Ibid.

10 Carol Memmott and Scott Bowles, "Film Features Author Cameo," *USA Today* (July 31, 2008): p. D2.

11 Valby, "Stephenie Meyer Talks 'Twilight.'"

12 Martin, "Meyer Watches as Her Vampires Rise," p. E12.

13 Valby, "Stephenie Meyer Talks 'Twilight.'"

14 Memmott and Bowles, "Film Features Author Cameo," p. D2.

15 Valby, "Stephenie Meyer Talks 'Twilight.'"

16 Martin, "Meyer Watches as Her Vampires Rise," p. E12.

17 Memmott and Bowles, "Film Features Author Cameo," p. D2.

18 Karen Valby and Nicole Sperling, "Fandemonium!" *Entertainment Weekly* (December 5, 2008): p. 24.

19 Ibid.

20 Matt Pais, "'Twilight' Comes Up Cold," *Chicago Tribune* (November 22, 2008): p. 15.

21 Joe Morgenstern, "'Twilight' Barely Sips at Juicy Vampire Genre," *Wall Street Journal* (November 21, 2008): p. W.1.

22 Jennifer Vineyard. "'Twilight' Author Stephenie Meyer Tries to Drown Jack's Mannequin in 'Resolution' Video." MTV News. http://www.vh1.com/artists/news/1594188/20080905/jacks_mannequin.jhtml.

23 Ibid.

24 Ibid.

25 Valby, "Stephenie Meyer Talks 'Twilight.'"

26 Grossman, "Stephenie Meyer."

27 Irwin, "Charmed."

28 "10 Questions for Stephenie Meyer."

29 Smith, "Author Interview."

WORKS BY
STEPHENIE MEYER

2005 *Twilight*
2006 *New Moon*
2007 *Eclipse*; *Prom Nights from Hell*
2008 *The Host*; *Breaking Dawn*

POPULAR BOOKS

TWILIGHT

Teenager Bella Swan moves to Forks, Washington, to live with her father. At her new high school, she meets the mysterious Edward Cullen, who just happens to be a vampire.

NEW MOON

Edward and Bella must part because his lifestyle is too dangerous for her, but Bella is heartbroken. She is comforted by her friend Jacob Black while Edward is gone. Every time she does something dangerous, she hears Edward's voice in her head.

ECLIPSE

Edward and Jacob Black join forces to protect Bella against a band of vampires that are out to get her, despite the fact that their kind (vampires and werewolves, respectively) are sworn enemies.

BREAKING DAWN

Edward and Bella are married and finally together, but an unexpected pregnancy leads to the end of Bella's human life and begins her vampire existence. The newlywed Cullens have to fight off the ruling vampire elite: the Volturi.

THE HOST

Aliens are slowly taking over the Earth by invading the bodies of unsuspecting humans, but one alien, Wanderer, encounters resistance in her human host, Melanie Stryder. As the two struggle internally, Wanderer becomes intrigued by Melanie's thoughts and feelings and falls in love with Melanie's lover.

POPULAR CHARACTERS

BELLA SWAN

Bella, the heroine of the Twilight saga, falls in love with Edward Cullen and into a series of perilous adventures involving vengeful vampires and warring werewolves but is able to hold her own and demonstrate her own special abilities.

EDWARD CULLEN

Edward, a perpetually 18-year-old vampire, lives in a vampire coven that only drinks the blood of animals.

JACOB BLACK

Bella's other love interest in the Twilight books, Jacob fiercely protects Bella and eventually gives her up to her true love, but he ultimately falls in love with her daughter.

MELANIE STRYDER

Melanie is a strong woman and a member of the resistance. She fights the alien invasion even after her own body is taken over.

WANDERER

Wanderer is an alien who invades Melanie Stryder's body and begins to love the people Melanie holds most dear.

MAJOR AWARDS

2005 *Twilight* is named as a *New York Times* Editor's Choice, a *Publishers Weekly* Best Book of the Year, and an Amazon.com Best Book of the Decade . . . So Far.

2006 *Twilight* earns a place on the American Library Association's Top Ten Best Books for Young Adults and Top Ten Books for Reluctant Readers lists.

2009 Stephenie Meyer is named Author of the Year at the Children's Choice Book Awards for *Breaking Dawn*. At the same ceremony, *Breaking Dawn* wins the award for Teen Choice Book of the Year.

BIBLIOGRAPHY

Books

Gresh, Lois H. *The Twilight Companion: The Unauthorized Guide to the Series*. New York: St. Martin's Press, 2008.

Meyer, Stephenie. *Twilight*. New York: Little, Brown, 2005.

———. *New Moon*. New York: Little, Brown, 2006.

———. *Eclipse*. New York: Little, Brown, 2007.

———. *Breaking Dawn*. New York: Little, Brown, 2008.

Ostling, Richard N., and Joan K. Ostling. *Mormon America*. New York: HarperCollins, 2007.

Periodicals

Bell, Carrie. "The 'Twilight' Premiere: Hysteria and Happy Campers." *Entertainment Weekly* (November 28, 2008): p. 9.

Braithwaite, Alyssa. "Fed: Is US Author Stephenie Meyer the New JK Rowling?" AAP General News Wire (July 25, 2008).

Carpenter, Susan. "Column One; Your Next Stop: The 'Twilight' Zone; Thousands of Fans Have Visited the Town Where the Vampire Novels Are Set. The Town Is Drinking It Up." *Los Angeles Times* (November 15, 2008): p. A1.

———. "Web Gave 'Twilight' Fresh Blood; Stephenie Meyer Grew Her Books' Readership with a Constant, Open, Grateful and Helpful Online Presence." *Los Angeles Times* (November 29, 2008): p. E1.

Crandall, Sandra Udall. "New Moon." *Journal of Adolescent & Adult Literacy* 51 (September 2007): p. 79.

Cruze, Karen. "Twilight." *Booklist* 102 (March 1, 2006): p. 105.

D'Ammassa, Don. "Twilight." *Chronicle* 28 (December 2005/January 2006): p. 31.

Deahl, Rachel. "Little, Brown Has Big Plans for Meyer." *Publishers Weekly* 254 (July 23, 2007): p. 19.

de Lint, Charles. "The Host." *Fantasy & Science Fiction* 115 (December, 2008): p. 38.

Dobrez, Cindy. "New Moon." *Booklist* 102 (July 2006): p. 51.

———. "Eclipse." *Booklist* 104 (September 15, 2007): p. 74.

Goodnow, Cecelia. "Debut Writer Shines with 'Twilight.'" *Seattle Post-Intelligencer* (October 8, 2005): p. E1.

———. "A Vampire Romance; 'Twilight' Author's Teen Fans Have True Love Flowing Through Their Veins." *Seattle Post-Intelligencer* (June 29, 2006): p. C1.

———. "A Bite of Romance; Stephenie Meyer's Forks-based Saga of Teen Vampire Love Is Now a Global Hit." *Seattle Post-Intelligencer* (August 7, 2007): p. C1.

Green, Heather. "Harry Potter with Fangs—and a Social Network." *BusinessWeek* (August 11, 2008): p. 44.

Hand, Elizabeth. "Love Bites." *Washington Post* (August 10, 2008): p. BW07.

Ives, Nat. "Making Release of 'Breaking Dawn' One for the Books." *Advertising Age* 79 (August 11, 2008): p. 7.

King, Susan. "David Strick's Hollywood Backlot; 'Twilight' Stunts Are a Cut Above." *Los Angeles Times* (November 20, 2008): p. E3.

Kirschling, Gregory. "Stephenie Meyer's 'Twilight' Zone." *Entertainment Weekly* (August 10, 2007): p. 74.

Kloer, Phil. "First Look: 'Twilight': Vampires, Romance and Hair—Oh My!" *Atlanta Journal-Constitution* (November 20, 2008): p. E1.

Martin, Denise. "Meyer Watches as Her Vampires Rise." *Los Angeles Times* (November 21, 2008): p. E12.

Meadows, Bob, and Kari Lydersen. "Stephenie Meyer Written in Blood." *People* 70 (September 8, 2008): p. 90.

Memmott, Carol, and Scott Bowles. "Film Features Author Cameo." *USA Today* (July 31, 2008): p. D2.

Morgenstern, Joe. "'Twilight' Barely Sips at Juicy Vampire Genre," *Wall Street Journal* (November 21, 2008): p. W1.

Nelson, Sara. "Breaking Trust?" *Publishers Weekly* 255 (August 11, 2008): p. 5.

"New Moon." *Publishers Weekly* 253 (July 17, 2006): p. 159.

Pais, Matt. "Twilight' Comes Up Cold." *Chicago Tribune* (November 22, 2008): p. 15.

Rafferty, Terrence. "Love and Pain and the Teenage Vampire Thing." *New York Times* (November 2, 2008): p. MT6.

Ramirez, Marc. "Vampire Series Brings Washington Town Back from the Dead." *Chicago Tribune* (August 17, 2008): p. 9.

Reese, Jennifer. "Breaking Dawn." *Entertainment Weekly* (August 15, 2008): p. 68.

Schillinger, Liesl. "Children's Books/Young Adult, Eclipse." *New York Times Book Review* (August 12, 2007): p. 19.

Stevenson, Deborah. "Twilight." *Bulletin of the Center for Children's Books* 59 (December 2005): p. 195.

Trachtenberg, Jeffrey A. "Booksellers Find Life After Harry in a Vampire Novel." *Wall Street Journal* (August 10, 2007): p. B.1.

Valby, Karen. "No. 5: Stephenie Meyer." *Entertainment Weekly* (November 21, 2008): p. 44.

Valby, Karen, and Nicole Sperling. "Fandemonium!" *Entertainment Weekly* (December 5, 2008): p. 24.

Ward, Kate. "Out for Blood, 'Twilight' Fans Bite Back at the New Book." *Entertainment Weekly* (August 15, 2008): p. 8.

Web Sites

"Amazon Exclusive: Stephenie Meyer Talks About *The Host*," Amazon. com. Available online. URL: http://www.amazon.com/Host-Novel-Stephenie-Meyer/dp/0316068047.

"Authors: Interviews: Stephenie Meyer," Young Adult (& Kid's) Books Central. Available online. URL: http://www.yabookscentral. com/cfusion/index.cfm?fuseAction=authors.interview&author_id=1564&interview_id=121.

Card, Orson Scott. "Stephenie Meyer," *Time*, April 30, 2008. Available online. URL: http://www.time.com/time/specials/2007/time100/article/0,28804,1733748_1733752_1736282,00.html.

"Fiction Reviews," *Publishers Weekly*, March 31, 2008. Available online. URL: http://www.publishersweekly.com/article/CA6545564.html?q=fiction+reviews+3%2F31%2F2008.

Futterman, Erica. "*Twilight* Author Stephenie Meyer on Her Upcoming Movie and Mermaid Dreams," *Rolling Stone*, August 8, 2008. Available online. URL: http://www.rollingstone.com/news/story/22493653/dawn_of_the_undead.

———. "Why Stephenie Meyer Gave Her Vampire Book (and Soon-to-Be Film) Series a Rock & Roll Soundtrack of Muse, Linkin Park, Blue October and More," *Rolling Stone*, August 8, 2008. Available online.

URL: http://www.rollingstone.com/news/story/22493653/dawn_of_the_undead.

Grossman, Lev. "Stephenie Meyer: A New J.K. Rowling?" *Time*, April 24, 2008. Available online. URL: http://www.time.com/time/magazine/article/0,9171,1734838,00.html.

"Home Page," TwilightMOMS. Available online. URL: http://www.twilightmoms.com.

Irwin, Megan. "Charmed," *Phoenix New Times*, July 12, 2007. Available online. URL: http://www.phoenixnewtimes.com/2007-07-12/news/charmed.

Lynch, Lorrie. "Exclusive: Stephen King on J.K. Rowling, Stephenie Meyer," *USA Weekend*, February 2, 2009. http://blogs.usaweekend.com/whos_news/2009/02/exclusive-steph.html.

Martin, Denise "'Twilight': Stephenie Meyer Lets Her Inner Fangirl Loose at the 'Breaking Dawn' Concert Series," *Los Angeles Times*, August 8, 2008. Available online. URL: http://latimesblogs.latimes.com/herocomplex/2008/08/twilight-stephe.html.

Meyer, Stephenie. "March 27, 2009," The Official Website of Stephenie Meyer. Available online. URL: http://stepheniemeyer.com.

———. *"Midnight Sun:* Edward's Version of Twilight," The Official Website of Stephenie Meyer. Available online. URL: http://stepheniemeyer.com/midnightsun.html.

———. "The Story Behind *Twilight*," The Official Website of Stephenie Meyer. Available online. URL: http://stepheniemeyer.com/twilight.html.

———. "Unofficial Bio," The Official Website of Stephenie Meyer. Available online. URL: http://stepheniemeyer.com/bio_unofficial.html.

Rose, Jamie. "The 'Twilight' Zone: Valley Author Thrust into Stardom," *Arizona Republic*, November 21, 2008. Available online. URL: http://www.azcentral.com/arizonarepublic/news/articles/2008/11/21/20081121twilightbuzz21a1.html.

Smith, Cynthia Leitich. "Author Interview: Stephenie Meyer on Twilight," Cynsations, March 27, 2006. Available online. URL: http://cynthialeitichsmith.blogspot.com/2006/03/author-interview-stephenie-meyer-on.html.

Spires, Elizabeth. "'Enthusiasm,' by Polly Shulman and 'Twilight,' by Stephenie Meyer," *New York Times*, February 12, 2006. Available online. URL: http://www.nytimes.com/2006/02/12/books/review/12spires.html.

Standlee, P.J. "Stephenie Meyer, J.S. Lewis and More Young Adult Authors Fight Cancer with Project Book Babe," *Phoenix New Times*, April 7, 2009. Available online. URL: http://blogs.phoenixnewtimes.com/uponsun/2009/04/stephenie_meyer_js_lewis_and_m.php.

"Stephenie Meyer," Fantasy Literature. Available online. URL: http://www.fantasyliterature.net/meyerstephenie.html.

"10 Questions for Stephenie Meyer," *Time*, August 21, 2008. Available online. URL: http://www.time.com/time/magazine/article/0,9171,1834663,00.html.

Twilight Lexicon Administrator. "Email Subject: Stephenie Meyer Biography," e-mail with Tracey Baptiste, March 5, 2009.

Valby, Karen. "Stephenie Meyer Talks 'Twilight,'" EW.com, November 5, 2008. Available online. URL: http://www.ew.com/ew/article/0,,20234559_20234567_20238527,00.html.

Vineyard, Jennifer. "'Twilight' Author Stephenie Meyer Tries to Drown Jack's Mannequin in 'Resolution' Video," MTV News. Available online. URL: http://www.vh1.com/artists/news/1594188/20080905/jacks_mannequin.jhtml.

Vogeler, Boyd. "Stephenie Meyer Sucks Blood out of Literature," Boyd Where Prohibited. Available online. URL: http://ebv.blogspot.com/2008/05/stephenie-meyer-sucks-blood-out-of.html.

"Walmart to Add 'Twilight Shops' in All Stores in March with Arrival of Movie DVD," PR Newswire. Available online. URL: http://news.prnewswire.com/DisplayReleaseContent.aspx?ACCT=104&STORY=/www/story/02-12-2009/0004971094&EDATE.

Whitworth, Damian. "Harry Who? Meet the New J.K. Rowling," *Times*, May 13, 2008. Available online. URL: http://entertainment.timesonline.co.uk/tol/arts_and_entertainment/books/article3917660.ece.

Wolcott, James. "The Twilight Zone," *Vanity Fair*, December 2008. Available online. URL: http://www.vanityfair.com/culture/features/2008/12/twilight200812?printable=true&currentPage=all.

FURTHER READING

Books

Gresh, Lois H. *The Twilight Companion: The Unauthorized Guide to the Series*. New York: St. Martin's Press, 2008.

Ostling, Richard N., and Joan K. Ostling. *Mormon America: The Power and the Promise*. New York: HarperCollins, 2007.

Web Sites

The Official Website of Stephenie Meyer
http://www.stepheniemeyer.com

Twilight Lexicon
http://www.twilightlexicon.com

The Twilight Saga
http://www.thetwilightsaga.com

Twilighters Anonymous
http://www.twilightersanonymous.com

TwilightMOMS
http://www.twilightmoms.com

INDEX

Adams, Douglas, 24
afterlife, 29–30
aliens, 79
Alma, Book of, 30
Anne of Green Gables (Montgomery), 24
Arizona, 22
Arizona State University, 16
Austen, Jane, 36, 69

balance, need for, 63–67
beauty, 84, 87–88
beheading, 94
Bella Cullen Project, 58
Bella Penombra fan site, 74
Beyond Boundaries Travel, 49
Bible, 30
bidding war, 40–41
Black, Jacob, 54, 56
Blade, 92, 93
blogging, 14
blood, 45
Bludworth, Katie, 74–75
Blue October, 75
boiling oil or water, 94
Bookazine, 18
Brandmire, Mark, 50
Breaking Dawn (Meyer)
  fans and, 16–17
  hybrid in, 92
  Mormon faith in, 29–30
  overview of, 71–73
  response to, 74–76
  reviews of, 73–74
Brigham Young University (BYU), 23, 25
Brönte, Charlotte, 36
Brown, Dan, 56
Buffy the Vampire Slayer, 35–36, 67

bullets, silver, 93
Bunnicula, 84
burning, 92–95
Byrne-Cristiano, Laura, 74

Café Press, 17
Card, Orson Scott, 24, 28, 69
Carpenter, Susan, 68
cereal, 84
Changing Hands Bookstore, 12–13, 16
Chaparral High School, 22–23
charm, 85–87
chastity, 28, 29, 45, 67–68
chessboard, 73
Chile, 24
church, 25–27
Church of Latter-day Saints, 25–27.
  See also Mormon faith
Collins, Barnabas, 85–87
Connecticut, 21–22
Corbett, Oregon, 49
Count Chocula cereal, 84
Count Duckula, 84
Count von Count, 94
cover design, 73
Crandall, Sarah Udall, 55
cremation, 94
Crohn's disease, 11
crucifixes, 94
Cruze, Karen, 46
Cullen, Alice, 55, 91
Cullen, Edward, 15, 44–45
Cullen Rosalie, 61–62

D'Ammassa, Don, 46
Dark Shadows, 85–86
Defining New Moon: Vocabulary Workbook for Unlocking the SAT, ACT, GED, and SSAT, 18

Defining Twilight: Vocabulary Workbook for Unlocking the SAT, ACT, GED, and SSAT, 18
de Lint, Charles, 78
Deseret Books, 28
dhampir, 92
Dobrez, Cindy, 55–56, 63
Dracula (Stoker), 67, 80, 85, 88, 89, 93
dreams, 12, 33–34, 39
dress code, 23

Eagle (dog), 21
Eclipse (Meyer), 29, 61–63
Eclipse Prom, 16, 65
Ell, Marienne and Annie, 47
e-mail address, 14, 16
emotions, 91
"To the End of the World" (Marjorie Fair), 58
Eulberg, Elizabeth, 18
Evanovich, Janet, 24, 37
Evans, Don, 27
evolution, 28–29
eyes, 87–88

fame, 65–67
FanFiction.net, 15
fangs, 90
fans, 14–17, 64–66, 68–69, 100
Firebird, 22
Forever Knight, 90, 91
Forks, 38–39
Forks, Washington, 47–51
Frankenstein (Shelley), 39
Fright Night, 93
Furstenfeld, Justin, 75
future, seeing of, 91

Gardener, Brittany, 15
Gardner, Erle Stanley, 79–80
garlic, 94–95
Griffin, Adele, 91, 92
Grossman, Lev, 80–81
Guckenberg, Bruce, 48
Gurling, Mike, 48

Hachette Book Group, 17
hair, 88
Hardwicke, Catherine, 98, 99, 100, 102
Harry Potter series (Rowling), 62, 80–81
hearing of thoughts, 91
heart, stake through, 93
"Hell on Earth" (Meyer), 66
The Hitchhiker's Guide to the Galaxy (Adams), 24
Hochhalter, Faith, 12–13
honeymoon, 72
The Host (Meyer), 78
Hughes, Janet, 48
humor, 63
hybrids, 92
"Hysteria" (Muse), 58

I am Legend (Matheson), 80
Ibbotson, Eva, 24
income, 13
Interview with the Vampire (Rice), 80, 83, 87, 88
Irwin, Megan, 63
Isle Esme, 72

Jack's Mannequin, 102–103
Jane Eyre (Brönte), 36
jewelry, 17, 48
Joffs, Lori, 15, 57, 77
John Wiley & Sons, 18
Journey to the River Sea (Ibbotson), 24
JT's Sweet Stuffs, 48
jumping the shark, 72

killing, methods for, 92–95
King, Stephen, 79–80, 84

lawyers, 77
Le Fanu, Sheridan, 88, 90
I am Legend (Matheson), 80
life, origin of, 28–29
Linkin Park, 57
literary themes, 43–44

Little, Brown, 18–19, 40, 71–72, 76
live, 67–69
The Lost Boys, 93, 94
Lutz, Kellan, 98

manuscript in progress, leaking of, 17, 76–78
Marjorie Fair, 58
marketing, 14
marriage, 72
Matheson, Richard, 80
McIrvin, Kim, 48
McMahon, Andrew, 103
merchandise, 17–18
mermaids, 103
Meyer, Christiaan (husband), 24–25, 66
Meyer, Eli (son), 25
Meyer, Gabe (son), 25
Meyer, Seth (son), 25
Midnight Sun, 58
Midnight Sun (Meyer), 76–78
missions, 24
Montgomery, L.M., 24
morality, 89–90
Morgan, Candy (mother), 21–22
Morgan, Heidi (sister), 37
Morgan, Seth (brother), 13
Morgan, Stephen (father), 21–22
Morgan, Stephenie (birth name), 21
Morgenstern, Joe, 102
Mormon America (Ostling), 28
Mormon faith, 23, 25–27, 27–31
Moroni, 27
motorcycles, 54
movies, 80, 97–102
Murnau, Friedrich Wilhelm, 89
Muse, 58
music, 37, 57–58, 75, 97, 102–103
MySpace groups, 15

nails, 88
names, selection of, 36
National Merit Scholarship, 22
Nelson, Sara, 75
New Moon (Meyer), 16, 29, 54–57

Nickerson, Steve, 18
Nosferatu, 89

obsessive writing, 34–37
Olympic National Park, 49
O'Reilly, Tim, 14
Ostling, Richard and Joan, 28

Pais, Matt, 102
Pattinson, Robert, 98, 99–100
pictures, 14–15
playlists, 37
Plum, Stephanie, 24
Polidori, John, 85
Powell, Mike, 49
pregnancy, 72–73
prom, 16, 65
Prom Nights from Hell, 66

Quileute Tribe, 54, 62

Ramirez, Marc, 49
Rancour, Carolyn, 67–68
Rasmussen, Emily (sister), 35–36, 37
Reamer, Jodi, 39, 40–41
Reese, Jennifer, 72
rejections, 39–40
"The Resolution" (Jack's Mannequin), 102–103
reviews
    of *Breaking Dawn*, 73–74
    of *Eclipse*, 62–63
    of movies, 102
    of *New Moon*, 55–57
    of *Twilight*, 46–47
Rice, Ann, 80, 83, 87, 88, 90–91
Rosenberg, Melissa, 99
roses, 95
Rowling, J.K., 62, 79–81

Salem's Lot (King), 80, 93
sale price, 40–41
salt, 95
Schillinger, Liesl, 62–63
screenplay, 99

The Secret of Platform 13 (Ibbotson), 24

Sense and Sensibility (Austen), 36, 69

Sesame Street, 94

setting, selection of, 36

sex, lack of. *See* Chastity

Shakespeare, William, 44

shape-shifting, 91–92

Shelley, Mary, 39

Shelley, Percy Bysshe, 39

shields, protective, 91

silver bullets, 93

Skurnick, Lizzie, 84

Slade, David, 102

Smith, Andrew, 71

Smith, Joseph Jr., 27

Solomon (King), 30

souls, 29

soundtracks, 97

spinoff books, 18

spoilers, 63

Springfield, Rick, 91

Squidoo, 17

stake through heart, 93

Stevenson, Deborah, 46

Stewart, Kristen, 98

Stoker, Bram, 67, 80, 85, 88, 89

stunts, 98–99

Subway, 48–49

suicide, 55

Sully's Burgers, 48

Summit Entertainment, 18, 98, 102

sunlight, 88–90

Swan, Bella, 15, 44–45

Swan, Charlie, 49

Tingley, Megan, 40

True Blood, 90

Twilight (Meyer)

   Mormon faith in, 27–29

   overview of, 43–46

   publication of, 12

reviews of, 46–47

soundtrack of, 97

twilight, significance of, 43

Twilight Cranium, 65

Twilighters, 58

Twilighters for Forks, 50

Twilight Lexicon web site, 15, 90

TwilightMOMS, 16

Twilight Music Girls, 58

Vampire Island series (Griffin), 91, 92

vampires

   beauty of, 87–88

   charm of, 85–87

   fangs and, 90

   hybrids of, 92

   killing of, 92–95

   special abilities of, 91–92

   sunlight and, 88–90

   in *Twilight* series, 45–46, 67, 72–73, 83–85

   vegetarian, 45, 90–91

The Vampyre (Polidori), 85

Vandenhole, Anna, 47–48

vegetarian vampires, 45, 90–91

videos, 102–103

Viera, Michelle, 17

View Point Inn, 49

vinegar, 95

vision, 91

Volturi family, 62, 73

WalMart, 17–18

Wanderer, 79

Weatherford, Kady, 15–16

web sites, 13–16, 50, 74, 90

Weitz, Chris, 102

Wells, Linda, 50

werewolves, 62

Wolcott, James, 46

Writer's House, 24, 37–39

writing process, 34–37, 63–67

ABOUT THE CONTRIBUTOR

TRACEY BAPTISTE is a young adult author. Her debut novel, *Angel's Grace*, was named one of the 100 best books for reading and sharing by New York City librarians. She is also the author of the biographies *Jerry Spinelli* and *Madeleine L'Engle*. Her other non-fiction titles include *Overcoming Prejudice* and *Being a Leader and Making Decisions*. You can read more about Ms. Baptiste at http://www.traceybaptiste.com.

PICTURE CREDITS

page:

10: Matt Sayles/AP Photo

20: Stock Montage/Hulton Archive/Getty Images

26: © North Wind Picture Archives/Alamy

32: © Edmund Lowe/ Alamy

38: © Lebrecht Music and Arts Photo Library/Alamy

42: Summit Entertainment/ Photofest

48: Ted S. Warren/AP Photo

52: © Lynnette Peizer/Alamy

60: Lester Cohen/WireImage/ Getty Images

70: Bobby Bank/WireImage/ Getty Images

74: Brad Barket/Getty Entertainment/Getty Images

82: Photofest

86: HAMMER/THE KOBAL COLLECTION

96: Summit Entertainment/ Photofest

101: Steve Granitz/WireImage/ Getty Images